MOTHERHOOD

May Cause Drowsiness

MOM STORIES FROM THE TRENCHES

A Second Edition Monkey Star Press Anthology

Tina Bietler, Kristi Campbell, Lisa Nolan

Monkey Star Press
Petaluma, CA

Monkey Star Press
POB 5343
Petaluma, CA 94955
MonkeyStarPress.com

Library of Congress control number: 2014916710

Motherhood May Cause Drowsiness edited by Lisa Nolan
ISBN 978-1-941682-07-4

Book Layout ©2013 Joel Friedlander, thebookdesigner.com

Book cover design by Lisa Knight of Designs Done Now

Cover photo by Tina and Bill Bietler

Monkey Star Press logo created by Michelle Grewe

To tired moms everywhere, WE GET IT!

What hath night to do with sleep?
—MILTON

Contents

Motherhood May Cause Drowsiness

Contents

Motherhood May Cause Drowsiness

Warning Signs You Are a Sleep-Deprived Mombie

Tina Bietler

One: You are a mom who consumes so much caffeine that your blood type is now C positive.

Two: In the morning, when your alarm clock goes off, you experience the five stages of grief (in less than two minutes).

Three: You forget to look at your day planner, to-do list, and the humongous calendar on the fridge that was there to remind you that your kids have no school and you need to arrange for daycare.

Four: Upon arriving at work you are wearing two different-colored socks and you shrug your shoulders. (Your colleagues should be glad you showed up fully clothed.)

Five: The refrigerator is full of 5-hour Energy drinks.

Six: Your purse contains several more bottles of 5-hour Energy drinks.

Seven: You are moodier than a teenage drama queen who just found out that her BFF slept with her boyfriend.

Eight: Certain commercials suddenly make you burst into tears.

Nine: You have memorized all the squeaky spots on the floor so you won't wake the children at night, but you are too tired to go to bed and you go to sleep on the sofa.

Ten: You are tempted to smother your husband with a pillow when he starts snoring in the middle of the night.

If you or someone you know is suffering from five or more of these symptoms it is highly advised that mass quantities of 5-hour Energy should be consumed during the day and the sufferer be allowed to pass out at night, if only for a few solid hours (because that's all the sleep they are going to get).

Dear Sleep, You Wily Mother

Kristi Rieger Campbell

Dear Sleep,

You're on my sh** list. We had a date last night *as we always do* (which is why it's defined in our contract as a "standing date"). I waited for you FOR HOURS. You didn't show up. I find your behavior rude and inconsiderate.

You'd better have a good excuse for last night and show up at my house tonight ON TIME. You're in breach of contract, pal. While I am permitted to show up for you when it fits my very busy schedule, it is *your job* to be there for me whenever I need you. That's the rule.

Force my hand and I will have no choice but to spend some quality time tomorrow with either your brother *Nap* or your renegade cousin *Pass Out.*

Weigh your choices carefully. At this time, I'm willing to give you another chance. That WILL NOT be the case again. You have thirty-three minutes to prove yourself worthy of my (mostly) life-long love affair with you—starting NOW.

Please behave.

Thank you,
Kristi

PS: If the exact time of our date is delayed due to the fact that I have been forced to write stupid letters to you reminding you of your duties, that is your fault, not mine. You'd better be waiting for me.

The New-Parent Guilt Trip

Annie Swingen

I was a new parent. I was a confident mom. I had managed to keep my son, EK, alive for the first six months of his life. I had it all under control. Or did I?

It's time for me to 'fess up. Here goes: I did not. Instead, I was hiding my insecurities. And there were a lot of them, so many in fact that I made a list and called it The New-Parent Guilt Trap: Questions I Asked Myself Before and After My Son Was Born. It is by no means a comprehensive tally of my various meltdowns and freak-outs before and after becoming a new mom (which will appear contradictory at times), but you'll get the idea.

Pregnancy Questions, Aka "What can I do before this baby is born to ruin his or her life?"

One: Did I drink too much before I found out I was pregnant? Will my child have a brain?

Two: Do I need to eat more vegetables or he will be in the remedial reading group? I mean, there is nothing wrong with the remedial reading group. Crap, I feel guilty for judging remedial readers.

Three: Should I eat less junk? Everyone tells me I am already a mom, that I need to think and act like one. But I love Coke, and Doritos, and Doritos dipped in Coke.

Four: Flax seed oil can go rancid. Good thing I learned that lesson after I consumed an entire jar via foul-tasting smoothies.

Five: What if my husband loves the baby more than he loves me? He already changed his ATM pin to the baby's due date. It used to be my birthday. Oh God, I am already jealous of my own fetus and he is only negative five months old. I am a terrible person for even thinking this. Still . . .

Six: What if I don't love my baby when he arrives? Right now I don't. I can't even sit down without being reminded of that fact due to the 400,000 pounds of pressure on my bits and pieces.

The New-Parent Guilt Trip

Seven: Why do people keep telling me it's good I'm not sleeping now because I am instinctively training my body for sleep deprivation? I hate those people. I hate them so much.

New Parent Questions
Aka "Welcome to the world, baby!"

One: Is my baby okay? Is he breathing? Check and see if he is breathing. Why isn't he crying? Why is he crying? WHAT THE HELL IS WRONG WITH ME?

Two: Everyone tells me about this rush of endorphins I should feel when I hold him. All I feel is terror and intestinal discomfort from the ice cream scoop of mac and cheese they gave me as my "first meal as a mom."

Three: Why does his face look like a smushed-up alien with my cousin's nose? Dear God, what if people think I had a baby with my cousin?

Four: Why doesn't he sleep? WHY, WHY, WHY? Humans need sleep. It's a fact. I birthed an alien-baby.

Annie Swingen

Breastfeeding Questions, Aka "If I don't nurse, does it mean I don't love my baby?"

One: Why won't he latch on? The smug moms told me it would be beautiful and natural and full of happy f'ing fairies. I hate those witches. I am a failure. I mean, he has been alive for 48 whole hours, and I haven't perfected this whole mother-son bonding thing. If I supplement with formula he will die because it's poison. Wait, it's not. I was on formula. But look at me now; inept. Yep, he will die. GET OUT OF MY HEAD SMUG MOMS!

Two: Why does it hurt? Am I doing it wrong? I was told it wouldn't hurt. I am a terrible person for thinking I should "give up." I don't love my baby enough. My boob is going to fall off.

Three: How does this nipple shield thing work? I should know because I have used one never, and what about the pump? It's supposed to be easy and provide my baby with a considerable bounty of milk from my boobs because that is completely logical to me. DID I ALREADY TELL YOU THAT I CAN'T USE FORMULA OR HE WILL DIE? I am insane and a failure.

The New-Parent Guilt Trip

Field Trip Questions, Aka "Look at me! I totally know what I am doing!" and "Forget it. It was nice knowing you, outside world."

One: Do we go outside enough? I know it's hot out, but if we just sit in one spot and don't turn on the AC (it's so expensive!), we won't sweat. Wait, the baby's face is red. Can babies sweat? Aren't they like lizards? Lord help me, am I cooking him from the inside?

Two: We go outside too much. Is he hot? Is he cold? WHERE IS HIS FACE UNDER ALL OF THESE BLANKETS?

Three: NO! He has real tears and is only four weeks old. Why is he so angry? I have ruined his life.

General Life Question
Aka "Have I lost my mind?"

One: I haven't written my thank you cards, and it's been two months since the baby was born. Except for the cards that I sent to the same people twice because I forgot I sent the first round. I am so tired. I need tape to hold my eyelids open.

Two: Do I hold my baby too much? Is he spoiled?

Three: I don't hold him enough. Do I love him enough? I must not. Loving moms hold their babies.

Four: Does he sleep enough? I am not sure of this because he is ALWAYS SCREAMING HIS FACE OFF.

Five: He sleeps too much and has plagiocephaly (flat head syndrome). He might need a helmet. I feel guilty about his flat spot. Good moms "wear" their babies. I was busy bouncing his chair with my feet while I watched old episodes of *Monk*. I feel guilty about caring what other parents will say about me when they see him with his little helmet. I feel guilty for feeling guilty because a helmet is nothing to be ashamed of. I feel guilty about not wanting to pay $300 for a test to see if he even needs a helmet. I am a failure.

Six: Was the alcohol milk test strip "dark" brown after I nursed him? I mean, the overhead light was sort of dim, so maybe it wasn't dark, but a medium brown? I can't tell! All browns look the same! Now I killed 5,000,000 of his brain cells.

Seven: Will scented wipes kill him? What about shampoo, sunscreen, fruit, vegetables (really any food), diapers, his crib, his car seat, and his toys? Should I keep him in a box? Will I be relegated to a padded room?

Eight: I showed up at the pharmacy clinic with a shirt, inside out, and covered in spit up. I am also pretty sure I took a nap sitting up while waiting for the LPN (licensed practical nurse).

Nine: Did I invite too many people to his birthday party? Now he will get sick and I'll have more thank you notes to not send out.

Ten: Did I invite too few people to his party and will he look back and think I didn't love him?

Eleven: I used a "birthday in a box" kit instead of Pinterest ideas to decorate for his party. Moms who love their kids make their own crafts. And organic, homemade cakes made out of kale and promises.

Someday I will make a list of toddler guilt-trip questions, but since I am currently only in the middle of that phase, I am in no rush to admit my daily freak-outs. With that said, this whole thing is pretty awesome (except when it's not).

My Child's Bedtime Lament

Lea Grover

I cannot go to sleep tonight
The sun is still up in the sky
My sister had more pie than I
My fingernail is scratchy.

I have to pee.
I have to sneeze.
May I have a cup of water please?
I need a Band-Aid on my knee!
I heard a doggy barking!

I don't care that I didn't nap,
Or screamed when I took off my hat
I've yawned for an hour-and-a-half
But I PROMISE I'm not sleepy!

Another song? Another book?
One with pictures! Let me look!

Lea Grover

Not THAT one, the one that I took
and left at Grandma's house!

I hit my head! I hit my butt!
Look! My thumb has got a cut!
The door made a sound when it shut!
Don't leave the room! Don't leave me!

I see a bug!
I see the sky!
I have an eyelash in my eye!
If you don't sit right there I'll cry!
Just look at me, I'm weepy!

Don't lean on that,
Don't sing THAT song!
You're doing all the voices wrong!
My parts are short! Now make them long!
I don't want you to be angry.

Just one more hug,
one more big kiss.
Here on my nose, that time you missed.
Teddy goes right here, like this,
Goodnight, sleepy mommy.

My Child's Bedtime Lament

I'll hum a song,
I'll whisper *hush*
I won't open my eyes up, much.
My teddy bear I'll gently touch
and nestle in my pillow.

The sun is gone,
the fan blades whirr
Here in my bed I gently purr
With little hands and growing feet
At last, your three-year-old is asleep.

In the Wee Small Hours of the Morning

Kathy Radigan

My house has recovered from another day of door slamming, sneakers running down hallways, couches used as springboards, and chocolate fingerprints decorating the walls.

The air conditioner is humming, and I can hear some occasional creaks from a house that is well used and well loved. No children are laughing, screaming, or asking for bowls of cereal.

"This is the time that dreams are made of," I whisper to myself. Or, more accurately, this is the time I should actually be *dreaming*, because everyone else is *sound asleep* (everyone but me).

I'm so tired during the day that I could fall asleep while standing with a cup of coffee in my hands. My eyes have such black rings under them that it took me a whole two minutes to realize that it wasn't mascara underneath them. But I can't give up my midnight rendezvous with someone I don't get to spend much time with anymore: me.

There is something about the middle of the night that is just too seductive for me to resist. No calls from my teenager, Tom, telling me he forgot the book he needs for English class. No calls from my husband, Joe, telling me his train is late again or asking me if we need milk. Not even a call from a school nurse telling me someone is sick or that a certain eight-year-old forgot to put on underwear.

All my chickens are present and accounted for. I take a deep breath and enjoy the serene feeling like a cool breeze on a hot day.

Some nights I just lie in my bed listening to the light music station that I adore or the comforting sounds of my husband's breathing that lulls me to sleep. Sometimes I catch up on a chick flick or old episodes of *Law and Order*.

But mostly I'm on the computer working or communing with other digital moms in blogger nirvana.

When I was growing up in the dark ages before computers and movies on demand, my mother used the hours after midnight to indulge her passion— cleaning.

In the Wee Small Hours of the Morning

As a young girl, I would go downstairs to get a drink of water only to end up scaring my mother as she scrubbed the kitchen floor on her hands and knees—too lost in her own thoughts to hear me approaching from behind.

My sisters and I bruised our shins so many times we looked like we lived in a combat zone, instead of a typical house in suburbia, all because we would fall over an end table that wasn't there when we went to bed the night before.

Mom, where's the china cabinet and the sofa? was a familiar way to greet my mother in the morning after one of her 3:00 a.m. redecorating fits.

I was shocked by how much that woman could accomplish while we were sleeping.

I loved the times I would find my mother wide awake polishing silver or cleaning out the fridge. She always greeted me with a warm, reassuring smile.

I could tell her about my day, or what boy I liked without having to worry about being interrupted by one of my sisters or a call from her office. I loved it.

Never once did she complain that I was interrupting her time or make me feel unwanted. For that I thank her.

She might even deserve sainthood for it because now I know how precious the hours between midnight and sunup are for a mom.

As tired as I get and as much as I may regret my lack of sleep the next day, I deeply cherish my nightly solitude.

The chance to think a complete thought without Peter asking if he can become a chicken or join the circus is hard to give up.

I also love to watch my sleeping children snuggled in bed with their dream-filled heads on their pillows. It makes my body feel wrapped in a warm blanket (regardless of the screaming fit Lizzy, my special needs daughter, had because she couldn't find her latest best friend or her purple flower hair clip; or what Tom said to me hours before that had me contemplating boarding school). Memories of my little babies lying in my arms fast asleep after a 2:00 a.m. nursing come flooding back—back when I could muster the energy from my mom-gas-tank just to hold and rock them. So what if rescue dogs had to find us under a week's worth of spit-up-stained T-shirts and baby blankets. It was worth it.

I promised myself I would never forget the feeling of holding my newborns in my arms or their sweet smiles when they napped.

The nursery furniture has been replaced by big kid beds; and two of those babies I once cuddled are taller than I am. In less than four years Tom will leave home to attend college, and then Lizzy and

In the Wee Small Hours of the Morning

Peter will follow in his footsteps. Sooner than I care to admit, my nest will be empty and I won't need the quiet of a house after dark to recharge my spirit.

I guess I'll sleep then (and remember to buy a better concealer for those under eye circles).

Go to Bed!

Tracy Winslow

Speaking into a microphone is Mixed Martial Arts Commentator Joe Rogan: "Good evening everyone! I'm here in San Francisco on a foggy Saturday night at the home of Tracy Winslow, aka the Petered Out Progenitor, and her two-year-old daughter Golden Girl. They will go head-to-head in a bedtime match-up *once again* tonight. The Golden Girl hasn't slept through the night in over two years and intends to keep this streak going for as long as she is able. The Petered Out Progenitor is close to retirement and does not recover quickly any longer. She is 'petered out' and ready to sleep for a month or two.

"It's not every day I get to announce that a world heavyweight championship fight is being broadcast live from California *right in the Petered Out Progenitor's bedroom*. Granted, it was challenging to get here: I tripped over a pile of toys and some shoes on the way in. But thankfully I fell into a large pile of laundry and was uninjured."

"Petered Out Progenitor and Golden Girl are taking their feuds to a new level, as the ladies will go head-to-head at bedtime, hopefully some time before midnight because, as the Progenitor says, 'She really wants to have at least one complete REM cycle tonight.' "

HBO Commentator Lennox Lewis speaks next: "I'm thrilled to be part of this event and I look forward to a really exciting fight on Saturday night."

Joe Rogan: "Lennox, what do you think Petered Out Progenitor and Golden Girl need to do to win this fight? What do you think the keys to success will be for each lady?"

Lennox Lewis: "Let's start with Petered Out Progenitor. She has to try and keep Golden Girl in bed and asleep. Don't give in to her demands to get out of her *kib*. Golden Girl is known for jabbing and keeping the Progenitor off balance. At 25 pounds of fury, Golden Girl is not a fair fighter: lots of dirty tricks up her Princess Aurora nightgown sleeves."

Fresh out of jail, Hangover Movie Mike Tyson: "Yeah. She does that weally well. Hey, what de hewk does Progenitor even mean? Is that what Arnold Schwarzenegger was in dat movie?"

Lennox Lewis: "Um, no. That's *The Terminator.* Tracy is Emmeline's mom."

Go to Bed!

Joe Rogan: "Progenitor has been slow on her feet as she prepares for this fight. It may be because she is in a perpetual state of sleep deprivation. Golden Girl should sneak into the Progenitor's bedroom in the middle of the night, tip toe to her side of the bed, thereby catching Pop unawares."

Lennox Lewis: "Golden Girl has a history of midnight massacre, including the now infamous bout in which she forced the Progenitor to walk across a battlefield of Legos. She is all no-holds barred and strikes when the opponent is weakest and often without her glasses, sometimes several times in one night. It reminds me of when I was Super Heavyweight Champion at the 1984 Olympics but with more ponytails and baby dolls."

Mike Tyson: "Wet's get this undew way. Boff of da opponents are sweepin (and hopefuwy wifout a tiger). Hahahaha! What? Why you wookin at me? No one got my back on dat? Damn. Y'all awe hawsh."

Lennox Lewis: "It's round 18 in the showdown. Who will win this epic battle tonight: Petered Out Progenitor taking on Golden Girl, live from California!"

A Hello Kitty Karaoke Microphone comes down from the light in the hallway. The moderator walks up on the frog step stool to address the cameras. Did he follow the house rules and take his shoes off at the door?

Joe Rogan: "Fighting out of the pink corner, we have Emmeline 'The Golden Girl' Winslow! Clad in a pair of princess jammies and what appears to be a baby blanket held on by a hair clip. Golden Girl is a freestyle fighter. She stands three-feet-one-inch tall, weighing in at 26 pounds. She holds a professional mixed martial arts record of 20 wins and two losses, with ten wins by whining alone! She is the current, reigning, and defending Insomnia Champion. Fighting out of San Francisco, California is Emmeline GOLDEN GIRL!"

"Annnnnnd in the paisley corner is Tracy 'Petered Out Progenitor' Winslow! Clad in an old Holy Cross T-shirt and yoga pants, five-feet-six-inches tall and weighing in at . . . did she just flip us off? Is that allowed? Petered Out Progenitor says she needs a good ten hours of sleep a night to function in society. Lately she is getting only two, which is causing her to get all Jekyll and Hidey. Tonight's competition is to settle the sleeping score and to see who comes out Reigning Insomnia Champion of the Mattress."

It's 2:00 a.m. Let's Get Ready To Rumble! Ding, Ding, Ding!

Go to Bed!

Lennox Lewis: "Petered Out Progenitor is not at all focused. This will not bode well for her entrance into tonight's competition. She is curled into a ball and can't find her glasses. Golden Girl makes the first strike."

Golden Girl: "MOMMY! Get me outta my kib!"

Lennox Lewis: "Petered Out Progenitor groans. Oh, that one had to hurt. Mommy rolls over and places a pillow over her head."

"Golden Girl clearly has the upper hand in this bout. She is lucid, having napped earlier in the day, and she secretly ate a fistful of pop rock candy that she stole from her big sister. She's small and wily. She has kept Petered Out Progenitor in a fugue of sleep deprivation, which makes Pop weak, shaky, and functioning on two brain cells."

Mike Tyson: "Yeah, dat was wike me when I got dis face tattoo. Sweep depwivation sucks, makes ya all cwazy."

Lennox Lewis: "Golden Girl is getting ready for her next attack. She scales the wall out of her crib and stealthily walks down the hallway. Next, she crawls along the floor next to Petered Out Progenitor's bed. The Progenitor is still all Petered Out from Golden Girl's last sneak attack. Golden Girl crawls up on the side of the bed. Getting leverage on the Ethan Allen frame, she leans in for the finishing touch. She opens her mouth wide next to Petered Out Progenitor's unsuspecting eardrum and . . ."

Golden Girl: "Mommy! Me are wake and not in me kib!"

Joe Rogan: "Petered Out Progenitor springs into action. *Finally.* We were wondering when she was going to show up to this match. Without a word she scoops Golden Girl up and takes her down the hall. Golden fights back, a swift kick, windmill punches, head butt, and an attempted eye poke. Golden Girl fights dirty. But Petered Out Progenitor is unfazed. This isn't her first appearance at this rodeo. Golden is deposited back into her bed without ceremony."

"Score One for Petered Out Progenitor. That's cool professionalism; it's what has kept the Progenitor going in this marathon battle. But Golden Girl has youth on her side, and a tiara."

"This second half will be interesting. A very loud snore emanates from Petered Out Progenitor's corner. That must be her coach, Animal Husbandry. Husband, also called Pop, is as always deep in slumber and unaware of the nightly battle waged in their boxing ring."

Joe Rogan: "Lennox, are you surprised that Petered Out Progenitor is this effective at her age? You know she's pushing 40 and still a contender?"

Go to Bed!

Lennox Lewis: "Yes. She's got a good diet and she's still got a lot of drive in her to continue, which is impressive. She also hates bags under her eyes—so that keeps her in the game. I've passed my prime in that sense, and I just want to do other things. My big show, as you know, was with you, Mike Tyson."

Mike Tyson: "Yeaw. Wemember when I bit your weg? Dat was high-warious."

Lennox Lewis: "The bell sounds for the second round to begin. Petered Out Progenitor is starting to show signs of wear. She is back in her corner and whimpering a little bit. She is looking for some advice or maybe a surprise tag in from Animal Husbandry but he's giving her the shoulder."

Joe Rogan: "Golden Girl is back on her feet. Petered Out Progenitor must be thinking to herself that it was a bad idea buying the 'big girl kib' that Golden Girl wanted. She can just jump out at any time. She saunters down the hall, the swagger of youth coupled with a narcissistic streak that only a two-year-old can pull off. Golden Girl wants to end this contest right now. She uses a ladder made of pillows, bed, and comforter to climb up and—wait a minute! She just propelled herself off the headboard, smashing onto Petered Out Progenitor when she was down. Is that even legal?

"Petered Out Progenitor moves a pillow and whacks it three times with a very weak arm."

"The round is over, folks. Petered Out Progenitor has tapped out. Golden Girl continues her undisputed championship streak. She takes a victory bounce and then crawls under the covers. She gives Petered Out Progenitor a swift kick in the kidneys, just to further demonstrate her superiority and then saddles up to her like a monkey backpack. Petered Out Progenitor clings to three-tenths of an inch of a king-sized mattress but is far too exhausted to care."

"Here is your winner, and still the Insomnia Champion—Emmeline the Golden Girl!"

Mike Tyson: "Poow Progenitor. She can't feew good about another woss. Dis makes it fwee yeaws in a woah. Maybe the Progenitor can come over to my pwace for some Tyson wovin' to hewp wecover."

Lennox Lewis: (laughing) "Ah, that woke up Animal Husbandry. I'm pretty sure you have been rebuked, Tyson."

Joe Rogan: "Petered Out Progenitor, how are you feeling after yet another crushing loss? Petered Out Progenitor? Hello? Well folks, looks like Petered Out Progenitor is unconscious. Place your bets in Vegas for tomorrow night when Petered Out Progenitor takes on the tag team of Golden Girl and Princess Ponytail. G'night everyone, for now."

It's Not Just You, Butterbean, It's My Melons

Allison Carter

I watched a lot of movies and read a lot of books about how my mushroom-faced newborn would wake me, wailing, every three hours. I was a disciplined student, and I had done all the homework plus some extra credit—I was prepared for sleepless nights.

When my *second son* was born, it was not my first time at the table, so to speak, and I knew with exhausted firsthand knowledge that there were going to be brutal, lip-smacking feasts for the baby at my expense. I expected my new butterbean to keep me up. What I had completely forgotten was that my melons would also keep me up. Yes, my own melons—my boobs.

We relished our nights in the hospital post delivery. We loved having extra hands to help us, people bringing us food, a TV right in the room; and I thought having a bed that went up and down with the push of a button was close to godliness. We were in no hurry to leave. With our *firstborn* we thought we could conquer the world and were eager to rush home to sleepless nights, frozen pizzas, tears of exhaustion, and "what is that cough?" arguments. But this time we had to head straight home because of those pesky little insurance rules.

On our third night home our new baby (number two) snoozed snug in his bassinet. As his second hour of sleep turned into a third hour and then a fourth, my husband and I snoozed for four hours: it was a sleep-fest miracle! Our baby butterbean was advanced beyond his days.

But then the other boob dropped. My milk came in—my boobs hurt in an aching, hot-needles-piercing sort of way. They throbbed and pulsated. I could not get comfortable. And I certainly couldn't sleep.

While my butterbean baby slept, I writhed in pain. I felt as though a geyser was about to spring forth from my huge breasts. Part of me wanted it to *happen already,* and part of me was terrified that all my breast milk would drown someone.

It's Not Just You, Butterbean, It's My Melons

You have got to be kidding me I thought. It wasn't enough to push a large baby boy out of my lady bits, but now I have to deal with gorged aching melons? And all the while my baby slept peacefully, but not me. *Life is cruel.*

At 2:00 a.m. I searched for home remedies on my phone: Google gave me cabbage leaves. That's right, cabbage leaves: "Stuffing raw, cold cabbage leaves into your bra, pressed up directly against hot, engorged breasts, offers a soothing remedy."

I will never look at this deity of a vegetable the same again.

As I poked my husband awake, I received an unsympathetic, tired, hazy, "wow, that sucks" moment of solidarity before his eyelids fluttered back to sleep. Humph, so much for being there in my moments of pain.

At 2:30 a.m., still in my pajamas, I decided to drive to our local 24-hour Harris Teeter grocery store. I walked stealthily to the produce section and grabbed one head of cabbage. By 2:50 a.m. I was in the checkout line.

I don't know what the clerk made of me in my flannel pajama bottoms stained with crusty grilled cheese, lactating through my T-shirt and nursing tank, and holding one lonely head of cabbage.

After I paid with cash, I rushed out the door, plopped into the driver's seat of my car, and tore that head of cabbage open in a mad frenzy.

I shoved raw, cold cabbage into my bra. I closed my eyes, sighed, threw my head back, and exposed my neck to the world. I felt bliss and sweet nirvana. Then I laughed at the funniest joke the universe and I would ever share.

After I returned home, I put new leaves on my breasts and rolled into bed smelling like foul cabbage. I snoozed beside my husband for fifteen minutes, and then my baby awoke, ready for some breast milk underneath sanctified cabbage leaves.

A Dose of Surreality

Shannon Drury

What do you get when you replace a distracted mother's morning Paxil with a tablet of Ambien? You get a mom who's more tired and depressed than usual. *Drum roll, cymbal crash! Thank you, ladies and gentlemen, I'll be here all day.* No really. I'm here all day. I have young children, and I'm not permitted to go anywhere. The real joke this morning is me, the sleepless and cranky mother who should have realized that all was not well when I lost consciousness while soothing my one-year-old daughter, Miriam, into her morning nap.

Our ritual consisted of two soporific books; Nick Drake's all-acoustic *Pink Moon* CD—at a low volume; and a long snuggle in the green chair in the corner of my daughter's room.

Miriam hated being plopped in her crib cold; she needed to be eased into sleep, to be held, patted, cooed at. I loved tucking her soft blond head into the warm space between my collarbone and my cheek and breathing into her tiny ear, as deeply and calmly as Buddha himself. This served as a daily meditation practice for me.

I was a devoted, at-home mom of two who wouldn't dream of doing anything as self-indulgent as, say, tending to her mental health by sitting in the lotus position for two minutes—not when my darlings needed organic snacks made from scratch; romps in neighborhood parks for exercise; flashcards in the hot language *du jour* (ironically not French, but Spanish or Mandarin); and constant, unwavering attention. Such inspirational mothering was so anxiety-provoking that I needed Ambien to sleep at night, yet so mentally draining that I needed Paxil to ward off episodes of existential despair.

So things were going great!

Back to Miriam: My daughter's naptime cries snapped me back to reality, but in spite of her racket, my surroundings appeared swirly and soft, peaceful and dreamlike. Since it was 10:30 in the morning, less than two hours since I'd downed a pot of strong coffee and my morning medications, I assumed I'd finally achieved a long-promised, spiritual breakthrough. *Well, I'll be, I just transcended time and space!*

Dazed yet thrilled, I plopped my whimpering baby back into her crib and stumbled into my bedroom to contemplate the infinite for a while.

A Dose of Surreality

Reality soon arrived in the form of my six-year-old son rapping at my bedroom door. He was home from kindergarten on one of Minneapolis Public Schools' biweekly in-service days.

"Mom?" he asked. "What are you doing?"

"Putting Miriam down for her nap," I replied.

"But Miriam's crying," he said.

"Oh," I mumbled, "is she?"

She was. Even in my stupor I knew this was bad. Amateur yoginis like me understand that nirvana doesn't have room for crying babies.

I lifted my head from my pillow and witnessed the bedroom walls wobble like enormous blocks of taupe Jell-O. *Did I wake up in a Salvador Dali painting?* Then I spoke incoherent babble that only Miriam would have understood if she weren't so busy wailing.

I lurched across the tilting hardwood floor and was struck with panic: was my interpretation of the afternoon's events TERRIBLY WRONG? Was I on a *lower* plane of existence, not higher? Had divine judgment been handed down upon me when I wasn't paying attention? Was it my fate to spend eternity suffering from vertigo while being screamed at by a hysterical, sleep-deprived toddler (all for the crime of giving my kids yogurt made with high fructose corn syrup on occasion)?

Elliott banged on the door again. "Mom," he said, "what should I do?"

I gathered the strength to pull open the doorknob and reply in a raspy voice, "PBS Kids."

He dashed away, thoroughly untroubled (being instructed to watch television was Elliott's version of "follow your bliss").

After stumbling for what felt like half a mile to Miriam's room, I draped myself across the crib frame and slowly, *verrry* slowly, patted her butt until she fell asleep.

I made it to the bathroom and splashed cold water on my cheeks, recalling what had happened days earlier. I had taken a brief trip to visit a friend in Boston. The night before my furlough, I crammed a "just-in-case" Ambien into my daily vitamins and medications bottle. (I was micro packing to save on the cost of a check-in bag.)

The next morning I gulped down the final pill from the bottle, assuming it was my morning antidepressant, not a powerful sleeping pill.

Way to go, Judy Garland.

PBS Kids and Miriam's nap gave me enough time to brew and consume another pot of coffee. When the caffeine met the anxiety-cranked cortisol in my bloodstream, I felt stirrings of resistance against the torpor threatening to consume me. Pharmaceuticals, hormones, and Starbucks French Roast were engaged in a war to conquer my cerebral cortex, and by some miracle I knew my children needed to be away from the front lines. The caffeine blast powered our drive to the Midtown YWCA, where Elliott and Miriam could be safely supervised in the Children's Play Zone while I planned to endure a detoxifying sauna in the women's locker room (a fast way to rid my body of its remaining zolpidem tartrate).

Clad in a sagging, last-season swimsuit, I gingerly entered the sauna—a dark, wood-lined room the size of a meat locker (and a perfect metaphor for the sauna's two occupants who were as naked and fleshy as any butcher's inventory with splayed flanks gleaming, untroubled, and silent). *Had I traded one hallucination for another?*

"Have a seat," one of the nudes offered. "Your first time?"

I nodded. (I didn't need to tell her about a sauna session in my youth involving parents who were out of town, a bottle of peppermint schnapps, and several semi-legal dares that I refused to complete.)

"It's really good for you, a sauna," the woman said.

"The heat," her companion added.

"I love it," the woman replied. "Your stress melts away."

"Mmmm," moaned her friend. Her white hair lay in wet clumps around her head as she rolled it with a white towel. "I am so relaxed I could fall asleep. Don't let me, Doris."

"Oh, I won't," Doris said, shaking her head gently, as beads of sweat dripped from the tip of her bulbous nose. "Save that deep sleep for after a good sauna." She turned to me. "You look like you could use a good rest, if you don't mind my saying so."

Was my judgment ongoing? Was I doomed to spend eternity in a sauna with two naked, painfully blunt old women? I had to blink a couple of times to reassure myself that I was, in fact, in a sauna at the YWCA and not in an extremely sweaty Hades.

"I don't mind you saying so," I told Doris, as slowly and carefully as if I were currying favor with Beelzebub himself.

That night, equilibrium fully restored, I opened up my bathroom cabinet, shuffled through Band-Aid boxes, ineffective beauty serums, B-vitamin complex, and zit creams, until I found an orange prescription bottle. I battled with the child-safety cap, and I flushed the little pink pills down the toilet. Goodbye darlings.

A Dose of Surreality

I have since given up Mother's Little Helpers for good. Instead of lying awake at night worrying about Elliott receiving a bad grade in Kindergarten Sandbox Cooperation (or that it would disqualify him from admission to Yale), I have a new sleep secret, one that occupies a special place on my bedside table and in my heart. It's a sleeping aid sans side effects that knocks me out every single time I pick it up, and best of all, it cannot be mistaken for anything other than a doorstop.

What is it? Why, it's Dante's *Divine Comedy* of course. I don't even reach the first circle of hell before I am fast asleep.

Motherhood Drove Me to Drink and Pass Out

Jessica Azar

Before I embarked on growing a tiny human inside me, I took sleeping late for granted: sleeping whenever I wanted; sleeping as late as I wanted; sleeping uninterrupted; and waking up alert and refreshed. Even if I had stayed out too late and didn't get enough sleep, I could catch a snooze during the day. So when I became pregnant, I thought I would have a nine-month reprieve from the impending sleep interruption that all seasoned mothers warned me about. Boy was I wrong.

For one thing, being pregnant made me sleepy, especially in the beginning. All I wanted to do was sleep all day, and because I had a full time job, this was not an option. You're not supposed to drink caffeine, said the pregnancy experts, so *how in the world* was I supposed to stay awake?

First, I tried forcing myself to take a short walk when I felt the sleepies coming on, but as I got bigger and more tired from carrying around extra weight, I turned to caffeine. Don't judge. (And I'm paying for it now with my oldest son who is a wild child because I infused his amniotic fluid with caffeinated drinks.)

When I gave birth to my first son, all I wanted to do was watch him sleep (when he wasn't demanding to be breastfeed or attended to, and even though I was exhausted from waking every two hours around the clock).

Everyone told me to "sleep when he sleeps," but after springing him from the NICU (neonatal intensive-care unit) after living there for seven days, I wanted to *take it all in.*

Besides, I was so overtired I couldn't fall asleep and visitors and well-meaning family members stopped by unannounced *at all hours,* which nixed any snack-sized snoozes.

And even though I was nursing, I wanted to be the one getting up to take care of our newborn *all night long* because my husband, The High Roller, had to "go to work" the next day. I was being a misogynistic martyr at my own expense, and I didn't even know it. (Had I known a huge switch would flip on within my baby, I would've taken sleeping pills and power slept for a week to build up my reserves. *Stupid hindsight.*)

Motherhood Drove Me to Drink and Pass Out

After a week of having the baby home, colic (aka The Devil's Scream) stormed into our lives, striking fear and inducing panic. I became a sleep-deprived, hormonal wreck, and I had no idea what to do with my baby (who screamed from midnight to four every single night for *three freaking months*). Nothing satisfied this child. *I am an inexperienced parent, so I must be a bad mother,* I thought. *Maybe he doesn't like me.*

The screaming wasn't limited to the wee hours of the morning. My new baby lost his cool the second something happened that he didn't like, or when his food wasn't served fast enough.

A couple of weeks into this around-the-clock hellish quagmire of care, I stopped nursing so that I could hand him off for a feeding. I decided to celebrate my return to the *adult world* by relaxing with some nice Belvedere Vodka on the rocks. (Yes, I'm hardcore. No, I didn't realize how dumb it was to drink straight liquor after being completely alcohol-free for ten months.)

I poured myself a double and left the baby in the capable hands of my husband, so that I could unwind in front of the computer, listen to music, and be left alone.

The first drink went down quickly and I was starting to relax, so I poured myself another. Yep.

I decided to listen to a Merle Haggard downbeat drinking song. *That was a good idea.* (It was not a good idea.) I kept listening to "Are the Good Times Really Over for Good?" on loop because it seemed to fit my mood of helplessness and fear that I would never have fun again, ever.

My father-in-law came over to visit that evening and I sat on my couch trying to intelligently discuss the stock market with him with a very thick tongue that kept slurring my words. At some point, and I don't remember how, I wound up back in my bathroom on the carpet in front of my vanity. I had the spins: it was the most god-awful feeling in the world. I felt as if I were on a tilt-a-whirl that wouldn't stop.

Then I cried. I cried because I was exhausted. I cried because I couldn't make the tilt-a-whirl stop. I cried because I felt like a horrible mother for cracking under the pressure. (And I'm no weakling: believe me when I tell you my kid could make a Navy SEAL crack under the treatment I endured.)

My husband came into the bathroom throughout my caterwauling to check on me. He told me to just "pass out." I knew he was right, but I kept fighting it and apologizing to him for being a bad wife and mom by getting myself so obliterated.

Being the control-freak problem solver that I am, I demanded he call the nurse's line at our baby's pediatrician to ask them how to help me sober up *quick* so I could feel better. I also insisted that he call someone named Pat Brown: I was positive that Pat Brown could tell us how to handle this situation. Neither one of us knew anyone by that name.

I decided that eating bread would make me sober, that it would soak up the alcohol in my gut. It was *another* good idea, so I told the High Roller to get me some bread.

Later, I woke up face down on the floor with an entire loaf of bread smushed under me. He must've brought me the bread just before I crashed down like Goliath.

The alcohol had finally slated my consciousness. And although I was still drunk when I came to, the spins had ceased and I was able to get up and go in search of my husband. I found him rocking our son in the nursery. My love for my husband grew a hundred-fold at that moment in time (as I tearfully stood there and apologized again for getting trashed and passing out). He reassured me that it was okay, that I was not a horrible mom or wife, and that he loved me. We both went to our room and fell asleep for a couple of hours, and then the baby woke me up and the High Roller had to go to work.

Later that morning, as I dealt with a screaming baby while recovering from *the hangover from Hell,*

I found a small note on my bathroom counter from my husband. It reassured me once again that he was proud of me and that he still loved me. It made me realize I could not be everything this baby needed, that I myself still needed to be taken care of, and that I had married the King of Men (sorry Jamie Fraser). I also learned that a mom can be driven to drink by colic.

Motherhood may have stolen my sleep and left me exhausted, but it also stole my heart and gave me more love than I could have imagined.

Seven Sacred Sleep Tenets

Cordelia Newlin de Rojas

One: If sleep deprivation turns you into a Joan Crawford cliché, sleep-train your baby as soon as your pediatrician gives you the okay. It's way easier to let an infant cry it out than a kid who can shout out your name and climb out of the crib. If your baby isn't in a crib, proceed to the next step.

Two: Turn off the baby monitor when you go to sleep. If your child really needs you, you will hear it. This does not apply to people living in mansions; you probably have a night nurse and/or nannies on staff. You too may proceed to the next step.

Three: Keep the room cold. Think about it. Do you want to get out of bed on a cold wintry morning? Exactly.

Four: Duct tape creaky spots. Use bright tape to help visibility under the cover of darkness. You won't regret it. You will become an acrobat, learning to catapult from one safe spot to another. When you feel ridiculous crab crawling and leaping across the floor, pretend you are a *ninja mama*. It helps, sort of. So does a glass of wine.

Five: If you need to wake your children, they will turn into 100-pound corpses. You can shake, jiggle, and tickle them, and they will remain asleep, their limbs hanging lead heavy. Similarly, if you wish to transfer a sleeping child from car carrier to crib, no matter how deep the sleep, he or she will wake as soon as you accidentally step on that creaking spot you forgot to mark. (Yes, I am nodding *I told you so*.)

Six: Forget "Shh, sleeping baby." Creating a quiet room for your child to sleep in will have you spending the next seven years panicking at every doorbell, phone call, and car alarm. You are doing your child and yourself a favor by teaching them to sleep in a noisy environment. A little Guns & Roses around bedtime never hurt anyone. My personal favorite: "Sweet Child O' Mine."

Six-and-a-half: Trust your instincts, and be careful whom you pick for advice. Best to go to mothers who already have several children. Beware of singleton mamas. They have yet to experience the fact that every child is different, and they are potentially self-righteous mothering bullies. (I speak from experience; I was nearly one of them. Karma got me the second time around.)

Seven: Sleep begets sleep. NEVER wake a sleeping baby or toddler, NEVER. If they are sleeping, they need it. And on the topic of needing sleep: DO sleep when the baby sleeps. Resist the temptation to get things done—aka the social media black hole where all free time disappears—while they are sleeping. You will be much more effective and able to juggle tasks if you've had some well-deserved shut-eye.

Finally, if you are unlucky enough to have one of the 20 percent of babies who suffer from colic, you will need someone to take over so you can rest. Nothing you could have done, ate, or yoga'd would have changed dumb luck. Be kind to yourself and ask for help. You are NOT a failure. You are amazing and made that little baby from scratch. Miracle maker, that's what you are.

With love,
Multilingual Mama

Too Tired for Goats

Kristina Cerise

I sat on the couch nursing my infant daughter while my two-year-old son ran around naked in my misguided attempt to potty train him. I was trying to adjust to a new life as a family of four. There I was, baby on boob and toddler on the brink of making another puddle on the wood floors, when the doorbell rang. I stumbled to the door, bleary eyed, only to be greeted by our backyard neighbor saying something about goats in my yard.

"I'm sorry, but now is not a good time for me," I responded politely. I shut the door, went back to the couch, and resumed nursing. ·

As I sat looking at my naked toddler while trying to keep my infant properly latched to my breast, the neighbor's words completed the journey from my ears to my muddled brain.

Did she say there were goats in my backyard?

When I was pregnant with my second child, I asked my brother (a father of two), what to expect– Would having a second child be twice as hard? Three times as hard? He paused, looked me in the eye, smirked ever so slightly, and said, "It's exponential." I was perplexed: Exponential? Like the curves in math class that start slow and then head for the moon? Would it be like an algebraic equation?

x = Workload associated with first child

y = New workload

z = Multiplier effect due to being outnumbered

$y = 2x * z$

Did my brother make the wrong word choice? I dismissed his assessment. After all, we come from a family full of linguistic quirks—we grew up dipping our fries in catsup, sprinkling powdered PAR-ME-SEE-IN cheese on our spaghetti, and eating oatmeal for "breffass" (nobody needs superfluous k and t sounds first thing in the morning). Blissfully ignorant, I waddled away and into the great unknown.

Back to the hungry goats in my yard: I walked to the backdoor to find three big goats eating the landscaping.

Turns out, our next door neighbor had fully embraced the quirks of northwest living and decided to rent a few goats to eat his backyard landscaping. I use the term "landscaping" loosely. Our neighbor cultivates blackberry bushes, morning glory, and other invasive species. Every three years he decides to do something about it. This year, that "something" was goats.

When they looked up from their prickly appetizers to gaze through the lattice at the finer, leafy fare in *our* yard, they broke down the fence and helped themselves to a recently landscaped buffet of ferns, hostas, rhododendrons, bleeding hearts, Oregon grape, and salal. It was a greenery smorgasbord.

I watched helplessly as my precious plants were consumed, my infant on my boob, and my naked toddler by my side.

Thankfully, the backyard neighbor was also a mother of two and recognized my inappropriate response to her announcement as a "new-mom-of two" haze.

She took charge of the situation and solicited the help of another neighbor. They chased the goats out of my yard and constructed a temporary fix to direct the goats toward the plants they were being paid to eat.

Nowadays, when friends ask me what it's like adjusting from one child to two, I tell them, "You will be too tired to cook, too tired to clean, too tired to form complete sentences—and too tired for goats. However, having two children will become a blessing. Eventually, you will look at your two kids playing happily and entertaining each other while you write, cook, or read, and you will realize that the *too tired for goats* moments were worth it."

The Family Bedlam

Renea Dearing-Dijab

Ah, the joys of co-sleeping, also known by sadists as "the family bed." Proponents of this lifestyle neglect to tell parents that every breath they take will be inhaled through a mass of tangled hair worming its way into their nostrils and, long after childbirth, a tiny foot will still be kicking them in the ribs.

Way back before I had a child, I said things like, "Babies are supposed to sleep in their own beds!" and "It's not healthy for a child *or* a marriage for the baby to sleep with the parents." What the hell did I know? I was an idiot.

My husband and I *tried* to put our daughter to sleep in her own bed. I think she was two years old before I completely submitted to her will and gave up any hope, like a doomed prisoner sentenced to life without parole. From that point on, she officially slept with us.

Sure, I would have loved a decent night's sleep, but I didn't want my baby to stop wanting my comfort because she no longer trusted that I would be there. I wasn't about to let her "cry it out" when she needed me (yet somehow I was the one who wound up doing the crying).

Our daughter chose to sleep *between* us, and due to her overwhelming need to be close to me and my breasts (before and *after* weaning), she literally slept *on my head* while mashing her face to my breast. Trust me, a good night's sleep is elusive when five pounds of toddler head rests on your eardrum, and the crook of a tiny elbow acts as a blindfold (but at least I knew where the rest of her body parts were).

The night usually began with one tiny arm over my neck and one tiny leg thrown over my waist in a human impression of "baby monkey clings to momma"—oh so cute in the wild, not so cute in our queen-size bed.

Sometimes she clung to my face with all four limbs, like a creature from the movie *Alien.* Other times, she shoved her head so close to my nostrils, that death by suffocation was very likely before sunrise.

Yes, my husband suffered the consequences too, but I shielded him as best as I could and took the brunt of it because he had to go to work in the morning. All I had to do was stay home and take care of my little soul-sucking vampire.

Occasionally, I would get out of bed and weep inconsolably and tell my husband I didn't know how I was going to *live* through the day.

It would be *years* before I'd achieve my right to sanity—and sleep.

Co-sleeping with my child was never my *plan*. It was more like *karma* for having had strong opinions about how people should raise their children before I became a mother myself.

When our daughter was five, we planned to move to a different state, and we thought this would be the perfect time to introduce the concept of her "Own Big Girl Room." We showed her a picture of a *five-hundred-dollar* loft bed. It would be a reward for sleeping in her own room. It had canvas panels, stairs, a SLIDE, and a turret that made it look like a castle. (Are you kidding me? *I* wanted this bed!)

She had to sleep in her room for one week before I ordered the new bed. My husband and I did not want to spend that kind of money if she continued to sleep on my head or choke me to death while I slumbered.

As we house-shopped in our new state, we turned down many a possibility due to the layout of the rooms. Her bedroom could not be on the opposite side of the house from ours. If we had any hope of ever sleeping alone as a married couple again, her bedroom could not be miles away from ours during the initial transition phase.

We finally found a lovely home with a Jack 'n' Jill bath between her room and ours. The door could be left open, and I could talk to her from our bed at night. I pictured us saying "goodnight" and "I love you" back and forth like *The Waltons*, until she'd fall asleep, then I'd spread out in the new *king-size* bed, limbs in every direction, reveling in all that *room!*

I am thankful we have moved on, but I am in no rush. I want to celebrate each milestone—with *plenty* of time to enjoy it before it's gone.

I am proud of the lovely child I brought into this world. (And I am happy to have my bed and my boobs back.) I'll be sleeping easier from here on out.

Wait, my now nine-year-old just asked, "Mom, when will I be old enough to kiss boys?"

Holy Crap.

One Night in Crazy Town, A Mother's Tale

Shannon Day

After two busy weeks visiting friends and family in the United Kingdom, my hubby booked a hotel room at the Manchester airport for our final night so the five of us could wind down after a very sociable vacation. Our three kids would have a bubble bath and we'd order room service and watch a movie together. Best of all, we'd get a good night's sleep and be rested and ready for our early start in the morning and the long day ahead. That was the plan, and it would've gone down had our four-year-old daughter, Mini, not fallen asleep in the car on the way to the hotel.

That night we had some pasta, watched a movie, and shared a few little treats. But when the time came to turn out the lights and go to sleep, Mini was just gearing up. The impromptu snooze, and a handful of chocolate eggs, had her completely wired.

With a large and mildly aggressive spread eagle, she claimed her sleeping position between her sisters, Zed and Ava.

"Owwww. Mini!" one of them cried.

Mini laughed hysterically as her toes probed her sisters' ribs.

After some quick adjustments, hubby crammed in earplugs, and he and Ava were set up for success. I, on the other hand, had sacrificed myself and was now sandwiched between Zed and Mini.

Zed tickled my back until she fell asleep.

Not long after that, Mini farted while doing a downward-facing dog. My time as the hostage of a four-year-old yogi began (and I was off to destination Crazy Town).

Overcome by giggles, Mini writhed like a crazed hyena. Then paranoia set in with ghost sightings and other random hallucinations.

Her legs developed a "sickness," and monsters stared at her with their fire-detector red eyes. She suffered a "weally, weally hot neck," which forced her to tear off her clothes.

She lost her vision for a few horrifying moments until tracing imaginary animals in the air brought her sight back.

She whimpered, claiming that "for weal, in weal life," something was stuck up her nose.

One Night in Crazy Town, A Mother's Tale

She blew snot into the darkness of the night in an effort to release it. I got her some tissue while she looked out the window and observed an earth-like planet up in the sky "all round, like a ball, with blue and green on it."

She laughed, then cried, then whined, then lashed out.

If I rubbed her back, she complained that I was "elbowin" her. If I said "Shh," I was mean. If I rolled over, she rolled even closer.

She then wiped her snot on my shoulder and told me stories that starred her as the most "impo-tant" princess in the land.

I was hot and sweaty. I felt tired and trapped.

And then, without warning, she passed out—topless and with a furrowed brow.

Sometimes our kids act like drunken fools and are prone to outbursts of affection and belligerence, determined to entertain, endlessly needy, and almost impossible to reason with.

Luckily, like drunks, all is forgotten in the morning.

(But the circles under my eyes tell a different tale of my night as a hostage in Crazy Town.)

Sleepless in Sanity

Kristen Mae

My husband and I pulled an all-nighter before we got married: we drove from Cincinnati, Ohio to Orlando, Florida, a 13-hour drive. I was awed at the man's ability to dispense with sleep. In fact, my reverence of his mental fortitude was one of the reasons I married him. So when the man that I had wed spent the first night holding our sleepless, newborn son and pacing the hospital room, I was not surprised. I thought smugly, *Golly, he's going to be such a laid-back Daddy. My shmoopsy-woopsies is the BEST.*

My husband banged his chest like a proud caveman and declared, "Pfft! That wasn't bad! I could do that every night!" And thanks to my post-childbirth fatigue (combined with the powerful pain killers I'd been given for my blown-to-smithereens-and-sewnback-up vagina) my addled brain agreed to my husband's suggestion that he be the one to stay up all night with our baby, Lucas. To me it sounded perfectly reasonable and not insane in the least.

Kristen Mae

The second night in the hospital went much the same as the first, though with considerably less pacing on my husband's part, and lots more sitting with his head flopped back in the ridiculously uncomfortable hospital chair, jaw hanging open in semi-sleep, furiously jiggling one leg to keep our baby in constant motion.

The next morning, my husband—in spite of having gone two nights with only a few brief naps while I breastfed—remained stubbornly committed to being the go-to guy for all-nighters. He was starting to look tired, but I was too worn out from the aftershocks of labor to dispute the issue (or any issue, for that matter).

The third day of my son's life was our first day home as a family of three. My head cleared somewhat, and I looked at my husband with a more discriminating eye: he now took on the air of an alcoholic hobo going into withdrawal. There was grunting and drooling and big tufts of hair smeared awkwardly to one side of his head.

We *thought* we understood the meaning of sleep deprivation before we became parents to a newborn. We didn't notice the red flags that began to show up soon after: like the day my husband cooked me macaroni and cheese and served it to me without mixing in *the cheese*. He served me noodles with only melted butter and milk, and it took me two bites before I noticed anything was amiss.

I sat in the family room, trapped and helpless in my new glider-rocker; unable to get up because of my aching, stitched-up privates; my nursing baby attached to my boob; and the bowl of hot, flavorless macaroni noodles I balanced on a part of me that wasn't occupied by a baby.

I couldn't get up. I couldn't yell for my husband (he was outside doing something *so extremely important* that it couldn't wait until my vagina healed), so I cried into my cheeseless macaroni noodles and hailed myself as The Most Wretched Person in the World.

It never occurred to me that my husband's forgetfulness was a result of exhaustion. I thought he was being an airhead, as when he threw his socks on the floor next to the hamper (instead of into the hamper, hello), or squeezed the toothpaste from the middle (who does that?).

Likewise, it never occurred to me that I was exhausted. Maybe I wasn't staying up two nights in a row, but I had endured 30 hours of labor and was waking up every two hours to breastfeed. Still, at the time, I didn't see our situation for what it was; I thought my tears of self-pity were purely the result of having to tolerate my stupid, airheaded husband.

I did my best to hide my exasperation. With clenched-teeth generosity, I encouraged my husband to sleep as much as he could in the afternoon so he could do his "shift" at night. It was probably the only time in our marriage since having children that I didn't begrudge him a nap. That evening, as per his self-inflicted obligation, my husband took baby Lucas from me, and we agreed that he would come wake me up when it was time for a feeding.

Two hours later, as I was sleeping the most profound and blissful sleep any human has ever slept in the history of humanity, I was suddenly, cruelly, jarred awake by the sound of our bedroom door being flung open with such force that it banged into the wall behind it.

"I CAN'T! I CAN'T DO IT ANYMORE! YOU HAVE TO TAKE HIM!" yelled my hysterical, sleep-deprived husband. He made so much noise it sounded like the Big Bang just went off in my bedroom.

"Okay! Okay!" I shouted back as my husband thrust a screeching bundle at me like we were playing a bizarre, late-night game of hot potato.

My first thought was, What the hell is THAT SCREECHING THING? Followed by Oh, that's right, I had a baby . . . and then HOLY CRAP WHAT DID WE DO?

"Calm down!" I snapped. My voice radiated with venomous anger after being callously ripped from my divine slumber. "You don't have to come banging in here. No one ever said you had to actually stay up all night with him! You volunteered, remember? All you had to do was ask me and I'd take over. Yeesh!" (No, that's not what I said; my word choices were much more colorful than *yeesh*.) I felt justified in my anger, and I truly believed I was in firm control of my mind.

My husband threw himself into bed with an angry "HARUMPH!" and yanked a blanket over himself, which fueled my anger more.

How dare he fall asleep while I was still pissed at him!

Our frustration with one another was caused by sleep deprivation and it made us insane. My husband manifested his insanity by being airheaded and forgetful. I got super angry.

There were days when I flat-out hated my husband for silly, faultless behaviors like clinking his spoon against his bowl, whistling too much, or breathing too loudly (or breathing, period). I felt helpless and alone.

Kristen Mae

If only someone had told me those moments of despair, rage, and misguided wrath toward my husband would pass; that there was an end to the chaos of sleepless nights; that I would feel normal again.

Or maybe the insanity of sleep-deprivation was something we had to experience for ourselves; a test to determine the strength of our relationship; a surly indoctrination to the brutal, marvelous roller-coaster world that was parenthood; and the belief that we could make it through anything.

Not long after the chaos had passed, I looked up to hear my husband whistling a silly tune for baby Lucas, making him smile and giggle that adorable, infectious laugh of his. I was flooded with a surge of love and admiration for my husband, the kind I used to feel for him on nights like the one when we made that long drive from Cincinnati to Orlando, except better because now we had Lucas.

My Little Squishy Face

Andrea Bates

Dear Three-Year-Old Daughter,

The three of us, including your Dad, just returned after traveling for two weeks, and we spent nearly every day together, which included sleeping in the same room each night. Upon returning home, however, falling asleep "solo" has become rough.

It has been weighing heavy on my mind and heart, causing me to question the choices I made during my days of early parenting, and I wonder if you will hold on tight and carry them forward?

When you were an infant, your Daddy and I did not let you "cry it out" (although there were nights when you cried and eventually fell asleep). We worked our way toward a better nighttime process, and as you settled in for sleep, I could leave the room and there was no crying.

Many times I've heard other parents say, "They're just babies. Take care of them. Show them they are loved, safe, and protected."

I knew that and I felt it.

Even on the nights when your Daddy and I yelled from downstairs with exhausted voices.

Even on the nights when one of us stomped upstairs and continued pleading.

Even on the nights I logged on to Twitter and scream-tweeted "FOR THE LOVE OF EVERYTHING THAT IS HOLY GO TO SLEEP!"

(Samuel L. Jackson sounded good to me on those nights.)

And I know that a burdensome bedtime hasn't done harm.

One day I'll get my late nights back, and not have to be awake until the wee hours so I can read and write; or maybe I'll catch up on some TV or go to bed early.

In the meantime, I will picture your beautiful face and dream of a strong future for you (and an easy transition into kindergarten, for you *and for me*).

You will make new friends, learn a lot, and enjoy yourself. You are going to be just fine.

And by then, Mom and Dad will have a pleasant bedtime.

Love,
Mama

Sleepless in Menopausal Motherdom

Marcia Kester Doyle

I never understood the value of a good night's rest until that luxury was taken away from me the day I brought my newborn home from the hospital. I assumed on our first night together that my son would sleep as peacefully as those angelic cherubs on the congratulatory Hallmark cards I received after his birth.

Ten minutes after putting him down in his crib, my son wailed loud enough to wake the neighborhood cats. He never cried like that during his hospital stay! The nurses swore that he dozed like a champion snoozer in the nursery.

My husband and I tried everything to get him to sleep, but nothing worked. What happened to my little Prince of Peaceful Slumber? He morphed into a creature of the night. I gave birth to a busy *night owl* at an all-you-can-eat *rodent buffet*, and there was no remedy to be found.

Well-intentioned friends suggested I nap during the day when my son napped. (My husband would not appreciate finding me in my bathrobe at 5:00 p.m. with the breakfast dishes molding in the sink.) There were no Keebler Elves who magically appeared to fold laundry or cook a four-course dinner. It was just me, my coffee, and my little owl. The good news: by the time my son received his high school diploma, he slept through the night (and some afternoons too).

I bore three more children and joined the ranks of other moms who looked like rejected actors auditioning for *The Walking Dead*. I had sleep deprivation written all over my face (i.e., raccoon eyes and duffle-sized bags under my lids) and would have sold my left kidney to the mob for eight hours of uninterrupted sleep.

Twenty years and twenty-thousand cups of coffee later, I'm happy to say I survived all those sleepless nights with babies in the house. I had to enjoy my slumber while my kids were adolescents because once they hit sixteen it was back to the mommy zombie days.

When curfews were missed and cell phones were off, I didn't sleep. When my kids first got their driver's licenses, I never slept. When noisy teen friends spent the night and trolled through obscure cable channels on our TV (or if they knew where our liquor cabinet was), I didn't sleep.

It has been ten years, and three out of four of my kids have grown and moved out to homes of their own. Now that I am past toddler sleep-attachment issues and bedtime meltdowns, you'd think I could get a good night's rest.

Wrong.

Mother Nature has a wicked sense of humor. She plays the middle-aged menopausal-mother card on me whenever I think I'm on the threshold of blissful, uninterrupted sleep. Thanks to Her, I have two new friends: Hot Flash and Mr. Insomnia, and they take sadistic pleasure in playing sweaty games of restless sleep roulette with me.

The shenanigans begin after midnight when Mother Nature cranks up my internal thermostat to match the temperatures of the Serengeti Plains. By the time I open my bleary eyes, I'm soaked in sweat and Super-glued to the sticky bed sheets. This triggers the "overload" alarm on my bladder, forcing me to stumble through the darkness to the bathroom.

Back in bed, I close my eyes and concentrate on returning to dreamland, but then I play twenty questions with Mr. Insomnia instead. *Did you turn off the stove before coming to bed? Lock all the doors? Bet you left your iPod outside and the weatherman predicted rain this evening. OMG I forgot to check on Jack's science project! Hey, did someone remember to walk the dogs?*

This one-sided ADD conversation continues for an hour before I am finally able to nod off at 2:00 a.m. Forty minutes later I awake to the loud rumbling of a freight train roaring through our bedroom. *What fresh hell is this?* I pop up and look over at my husband. He's snoring peacefully beside me, his lips fluffing out with each whistling exhale. My accusatory glare is wasted on his sleeping form, so I elbow him awake.

"Stop snoring! You're keeping me up!"

He mumbles an apology and slaps a Breathe Right strip across his nose, which makes him look like Muhammad Ali in the boxing ring.

After a few minutes he spoons against me and fondles my backside. *For the love of all that is holy, I JUST WANT SLEEP!*

My husband grumbles something incoherent and rolls back over to his side of the bed. I marvel at his ability to fall asleep in seconds. I count cracks in the ceiling for another hour until my lids close. Just as I am nodding off, the mattress shakes like a coin operated, vibrating bed in a cheap motel room. Did I forget to mention that my husband has restless leg syndrome? He rubs his legs together like a cricket and kicks field goals in his sleep. His constant twitching, kicking, snoring, and farting make me want to kick his Muhammad Ali ass out of the bed.

At that moment my body breaks out into a vicious sweat, as if I'm being tossed onto a pit of burning coals. I frantically kick off the blankets and crawl under the ceiling fan for relief.

And then the cycle starts all over again with bladder demands, the sticky sheets, and the snoring husband. His legs aren't the only thing that's twitching. My brain doesn't know where the off switch is. Does anyone remember if I left the milk carton out on the counter?

Sleeping Vicariously

Rachel Demas

Our babysitter came over at 5:00 p.m. and announced that it was her birthday. For a second I was confused: *Why is she here? Shouldn't she be out celebrating the night away?* Then she added, "After I leave here at eight, I'm going to take a nap and then my friends are taking me out." *Ah, youth. I had nearly forgotten.*

How nonchalantly our sitter mentioned sleep. She's twenty-one; she's not a mom.

I found her lack of reverence for shut-eye breathtaking. She announced taking a nap at night as if it were a given. It signified the ability to rest with abandon, to run fast and loose with snoozing like a profligate. She might as well have discussed inhaling and exhaling, instead of what slumber has become for me—an exotic treasure.

Annie's off-the-cuff observations often stop me in my tracks (pardon the clichés). One time I asked about her trip home to visit family. She came out with this beaut': "I only got to lie out once."

Lie out? First, I don't need any more wrinkles, thank you very much, *Ms. Flawless Twenty-Something Skin Girl.* Second, do you know how much I would give for the time to lay my body in a horizontal position in the sun with the *sole responsibility* of baking my front and backside evenly (and, dare I say it, sleeping)?

I think about sharing how different our perspectives are, but I know she wouldn't understand. So I nod as if I'm commiserating about the horrible tragedy that befell her while she sat at home and cursed the gray skies above.

I understand her. I was twenty-one once. When I was that age, I had long stretches of time to fill at my leisure. Napping was something I took for granted— and tan lines were a major preoccupation.

She can't comprehend how something as commonplace as a sun-worshipping siesta is a huge indulgence for the mom of a toddler, as it should be. I didn't grasp what an overwhelming, nonstop responsibility a child was until I became a mom.

The funny thing is I don't feel jealous of her carefree ways (certainly not the "lying out" bit). Being twenty-one may mean there is a world of possibility ahead, but I also remember a lot of confusion about what direction to take in life and the many missteps I took.

I can appreciate the privilege of youth without wanting to go back. As bizarre as it sounds, I feel more rested just thinking about napping after dark.

Cold Night Song
(Lullaby for Nana)

Shittu Fowora

Oh Ummu
Oh Onono Nana,
Oh cold
Oh fever
Oh flu!

Have you ever thought about immunizations
before you became a Mum?

Who dared puke on you,
poop on you,
chewe on you,
or pee on
and droole on you
    . . . before you became a Mum?

You had your mind and thoughts in place
you had your heart and body firm with grace

Shittu Fowora

And at night you slept all through
till first light of day
all before you were a mum.

Now you contend with stings and spasms
screaming and tears and hiccupy sessions
you are now a nursing doctor,
running tests between your palms
and his body, collecting innate reflexes

How he makes your eyes water with happy tears
how his chuckles make you grin with glee
and such is the gift that comes with the office

Oh cold
Oh fever
Oh flu!
Oh Nana, the Princess of Oak Town
who sits up into the night watching mustafa[1] sleep

What if I weave you a verse and make it into a neck-
lace
what if I interlace your hair into a prayer ponytail
How many will stand while the world reclines in bed,
all because you hold a sleeping baby,
because you don't want to put him down.

Cold Night Song (Lullaby for Nana)

How could you have known,
someone so small could touch your life so much;
cause you joy and cause you to dance
cause you pain, and sweet relief
don't you just love being a wonderful Mommy?

Using the thirteen colours of a bride's veil
and fullness of white clouds
I weave into words to lull you to sleep

Oh flu!
Oh injections
Oh immunizations
Oh weather

How are you to know the design between warmth
and love
and joy and eye aches and nose aches and heart
aches,
and the divine splendour and satisfaction of being a
Mamma?

Oh flu!
Oh weather
Oh croaking tadpoles

Shittu Fowora

Oh the breezy night wind,
be still for my princess seeks sleep
my ecstatic song shall halo around you
my words shall feel the pulsation of your chest
as I whisper you riddles and kisses with prayers,
wishes in warmth and a gentle feel of your cheeks
. . . sleep until the athan^2 sounds again.

1. [In Arabic, *mustafa* means The Chosen One.]
2. [In Arabic, athan is a call for prayer.]

Why Moms Are Too Tired for Sex

Lisa Nolan

How many of us moms does it take to screw in a light bulb? None! We are too tired to screw with light bulbs. It's the last item on our to-do list, the chore that never gets done, except maybe on birthdays or anniversaries. Did I say chore? Since when did fooling around with our husbands become a chore? And you thought I was talking about light bulbs!

Let's face it, the lights are dim. Heck, the lights aren't even on. Our light bulbs are burnt out!

After four years of marriage and the birth of one baby boy, my light switch gets turned on once every month. I used to feel guilty about it and oh-so-sorry for my husband. I've even considered having pity sex with him, but have stopped short of that because pity sex turns into bad sex; and no sex is better than bad sex; and bad sex would just make my husband feel guilty; so why make my husband feel bad? Huh?

The point is my husband and I don't have bad sex. In fact, we have great sex—just not that often. *But why?* I'm always asking myself. When did my libido decide to adopt a bunch of clichés: to take a hike, to fly the coop, to disappear into thin air? When the new love of my life was born! Who needs lovemaking when you have a brand new baby!

After the birth of my son, it was obvious my husband and I weren't going to do it for a while—then a while turned into many months. During that time it was easy to blame my low libido on breast feeding. *Breast feeding causes low libido,* warned my OBGYN. But now that my baby is becoming a toddler, I no longer breast feed him—so why do I have such a lack of interest in sex?

For starters, my body isn't the same as it was; I had an eight-pound, twelve-ounce baby yanked out of me; I grew a jelly roll around my midsection (no matter how many sit-ups I don't do); and did I mention my sagging melons? I'm saggy and baggy and won't let my husband see me naked anymore.

There is the all-consuming mommy to-do list. Before I became a mom, my to-do list was not only shorter, it was way more exciting: getting my hair styled, buying all the makings of a terrific dinner for two, and finding some sexy underwear at Victoria's Secret.

Today my mommy to-do list includes washing my hair (it's been three days!); buying another black T-shirt in extra large—big enough to cover my baggy, saggy body and dark enough to hide the spit up, dirty handprints, and general yuck that comes from all of my baby's orifices; ordering take-out for dinner; not to mention de-crusting the stroller, buying flea collars for my neglected cats, and checking my bid on eBay for the cutest pair of little boy's overalls you ever saw!

Then there is my daily mommy routine: picking up the pots and pans, Tupperware, measuring cups, and whatever else my son has managed to grab out of the bottom cupboards and toss around on the kitchen floor for the twentieth time; making a healthy, yummy nutritious snack that I hope my son will love, only to have him throw it on the rug, then picking up pieces of goodness-knows-what off the carpet; stacking an endless supply of sippy cups, suction bowls that don't stick, bottles, and tiny spoons into the dishwasher; climbing Mt. Laundry to get to the washer and dryer and take care of the dirty clothes; watching a soap opera while my son attempts to take his nap; and it's not even two o-clock! *Did I eat lunch yet?*

At two we either go to our playgroup, go to the park, take a walk, or go on a playmate, and so my routine continues with packing a snack, checking the diaper bag, and remembering to bring water (because we moms never drink enough water).

Upon arriving at home, it's time to feed my son a snack, check my e-mail, and straighten up the house—only to have it disheveled minutes later when my son is done eating and goes exploring. Soon my husband is home and the tossing of mail, car keys, shoes, socks, newspapers, and magazines begins, first by my husband, who is oblivious to the disarray of toys, papers, and various items my son has clutched from tabletops and bookshelves—and then there is more tossing by my son!

My husband and I exchange chitchat: How was your day? What should we have for dinner? Can you take the garbage out? At this point my husband scoops up our son and begins the father son roughhouse ritual that gives me a ten-minute break. But with only ten minutes to myself, I don't know what to do or where to begin! So I sit on the couch, watch the last of an Oprah rerun, and laugh at my son's grinning and giggling as my husband gallops around the living room with our little boy atop his shoulders.

I am also the cook in the household. I enjoy cooking. And since the birth of our son, cooking gives me yet another break from my mommy duties. However, I can't (or won't) cook dinner until the pots from the night before are washed, usually by my husband, who always seems to need reminding. But first our son gets his dinner, so I prepare his last meal of the day and feed him while my husband washes some pans; and then my husband or I attempt to put him in his pajamas, read a bedtime story, and put him to bed.

By 8:30 p.m. we are done with dinner, and thoughts of tomorrow begin creeping into my brain: Jason has a doctor's appointment at 10 a.m. We need more cat litter. I have five people interested in our walker for sale on Craigslist. I need to work on my paper for my writers' salon.

As I sit on the couch working out all the details of tomorrow, I scan the living room and tell myself to just leave the mess, to ask my husband to tidy it up— which he always agrees to do but then forgets as he falls asleep on the couch watching his favorite sports team; so I get up and begin to put things back in order.

By 9 p.m. my body is tired and done for the day. My mommy brain is short circuited, ready to shut down. I need *my time*, with no demands made on me, which usually means taking a shower, crawling onto the sofa, and curling up with a good novel from my

Lisa Nolan

mommy book club. Soon it's time for bed. But wait! There's one more thing I forgot to cross off my to-do list: put a light bulb in the socket and turn the switch on, or put it on my list for tomorrow, and tomorrow, and tomorrow. But, lately, tomorrow never comes—pun intended.

My Two-Year-Old Is Plotting My Untimely Demise

Tracy Winslow

My two-year-old is trying to kill me. She'll get away with it because she's so adorable—and tiny and blonde—that no one would accuse her of such atrocities. She'll blink her beautiful blues at the "powice" and run away to perform "fips" on the trampoline. And, it's all just one big scam.

Here's how I know it's going to happen.

1. My toddler has kept me awake each night for a month. She wakes up at hourly intervals and screams "Mumma! Get me outta dis kib!" If I oblige her, she wants me to "wock" her, pretends to fall back to sleep, and then freaks out if I put her back into her crib. If I ignore her, she screams until I'm certain the neighbors have called the police. She'll claim self-defense or neglect or abuse, or something genius, because I let her cry in her "kib" instead of

"wocking" her. I'm so overtired I won't see it coming.

2. I caught her drinking Hello Kitty lotion. Right out of the bottle. Who does that? Serial killers, that's who.

3. She booby trapped her room to either kill me or break my leg, so I could die a slow, painful death. The floor in front of the crib was full of Legos and pointy things, which were probably shards of glass. I'd asked her before bed if she had put all her toys away. She said "me did," but clearly "me didn't." Later, she screamed as if she were in a pit of vipers. When I ran in, I almost killed myself. Thankfully, I always wear flip flops and just ended up twisting my ankle and foiling her plan.

4. She caught "a bug" and brought it over to show me. It was a live hornet. And it was all kinds of pissed off because she was holding it by the wings. It was wiggling its bee butt trying to sting her. Honest to God!—This really happened. And I am allergic to bee stings. Thankfully my husband swatted her weapon of mild anaphylaxis out of her little kid fists and stepped on it before it could come and try to kill me. Again, genius, because the BEE would take the fall.

5. Once I caught her drinking toothpaste out of the toothpaste-holder-thingy, with NOTHING to

wash it down. Who does that? Criminal master-minds, that's who.

6. She wears pink sparkly lip gloss on her fore-head. Not necessarily indicative of a future crime spree, but strange nonetheless.

7. She is trying to starve me to death. Every time we sit down to eat, she wants my food—even if she has the exact same food (even if I trick her and give her mine first). Then she wants to sit on my "yap" so that any possible chance of food getting anywhere near my mouth is thwarted. In order to combat this, I have built up a large layer of fat to survive. Kind of like a bear in hibernation.

Yeah, she's coming for me. Or, maybe she's just two years old. It's hard to say. (Not that it's hard to say that she's two, I have her birth certificate.) But, if all of a sudden I "disapew" don't totally count her out.

The Long Road

Lauren Stevens

When my husband and I found out we were having a boy, a close friend of mine told me to get a good pair of running shoes because I was going to need them. I laughed and thought to myself, *I got this.*

After our son Declan was born, we were fueled by euphoria, forsaking sleep, and taking shifts to watch our new baby around the clock, lest he stop breathing (he didn't) or some major milestone occurred (it didn't).

Trips out of the house were opportunities for us to shake off new-parent cabin fever and show our little one off with pride. Soon, we were bombarded with questions including, "Was our baby sleeping through the night?" We'd politely smile, shake our heads, and proceed to tell those kind folks and well-meaning strangers our newborn was soiling 12 to 15 diapers a day, smiling at us (and NO, it was NOT just gas), eating nonstop during his wakeful hours, and cooing with gusto.

Within eight months, however, the "sleeping through the night" question (and all of the unsolicited advice that came along with it) began to wear me down, and all I could do was grimace, shake my head, and mumble that my son was constantly hungry and a lousy sleeper.

There was so much I didn't know about being a parent. After months of following my son's cues, I let him dictate the rules of sleep; I had no idea that I should be working with him on a schedule. My little guy had the upper hand and was unknowingly dictating every aspect of our lives. Naps were for wimps, and Declan would have none of that nasty business; real boys stayed awake to take part in life, not sleep the day away. Bedtime? Pffft! Bedtime was for sissies.

Soon I resented those moms whose babies slept through the night; surely it was because they formula fed their infants and let them sleep in their swings for hours. I was lucky to grab two solid hours of sleep before my son woke in the night for a feeding and I began dreading them.

I called my husband at least once a week in tears, having mini-breakdowns and blubbering on about sleep and other nonsense. I resented the fact that he slept on another floor, so that he could be well-rested for work. The sounds of my husband's snores taunted me as I sat rocking and nursing our son in the wee hours of the morning.

I began to fear nights. I became a shell of my former self, constantly at the beck and call of our tyrannical infant son. With my sleepless brain constantly misfiring signals, I was weepy and depressed. I was unable to understand how I could be amazing in my career, but complete bunk when it came to being a mother. I felt like a complete sham. Losing my sense of self, I could no longer see the end goal or the finish line amidst never-ending nights. What the hell was I doing? This sprinter needed to come to grips with the journey that was parenting.

I convinced my husband to invest in a sleep consultant after I forgot to buckle my son's carrier into my car twice, while out running errands. (Thankfully, we did not get into an accident.) I was waving my white flag, unable to see the finish line: my world had become a haze of endless days lived in slow motion. Sleep training it would be, and my husband was on board.

This had better work, I thought, or I would remain a crazed insomniac.

Paranoid, distrustful, and wary, I listened to our sleep consultant. I was shocked to discover that I was the reason for my son's wakeful nights.

She continued on about the importance of creating a customized plan.

Tired, defeated, but not completely crushed by this blow, I took the paperwork with detailed instructions, thanked our consultant, and made a pact with my husband to start sleep training the next weekend.

Part of the plan was for my husband to take over nights (yay!). Exhausted, I climbed the stairs to the third floor that night, sure that my husband would wake me to enlist my help.

I awoke in a panic six hours later, my breasts threatening to explode, unsure of where I was and what had happened. Sleep! Sleep had happened! The baby was alive, my husband was alive, and I had slept —hallelujah!

My son went from a non-napping, non-sleeping tyrant, to a baby who napped for more than thirty minutes at set times throughout the day and slept for *thirteen hours* at night.

My only regret from those first eight months of motherhood (apart from having few memories as a result of my sleep-deprived state) is viewing parenthood as a sprint, focused on the multiple "finish lines" those early milestones represented. Once I began getting healthy sleep, I came to realize that parenting is like distance running, requiring stamina, and made beautiful by taking the time to enjoy the beauty in the moments that make up the journey.

Each night, when I head in for those hard-earned eight hours, I remain grateful to be on this long road that is parenthood (and not a sprint to the finish line).

Don't Skip Naptime, Just Don't, Ever

T. Dawn Daum

It's the afternoon, and I'm nervously sitting in the waiting room watching my toddler ram toy cars into the walls. He missed his nap today because his sister had an appointment with the doctor. (His destructive behaviors are enough to handle on a good day; today could be the day his skin turns green and he explodes out of his Baby Gap tee because I tell him not to do something.)

I beg-ask my son to please not bang the cars into the walls, then a car flies across the room, missing someone's grandmother by six inches. (Now cue flopping fish-out-of-water syndrome.) I should have grabbed the volatile little hulk and his sister, and gotten the hell out of there.

The nurse calls us in, which distracts my tired, mini psychopath toddler, and all is cool for the next thirty seconds.

As the nurse tries to get my daughter's weight, Little Man is jumping on and off the scale, reveling in the aggravation he is causing. I swoop him up and pretend I can control this little human being. I put him in my lap and he screams, "Dooooown!" while the nurse attempts to get his sister's blood pressure for the third time.

Now we are in our assigned room. My daughter starts to undress and put on the gown set out for her. Little Man kicks off his shoes and pulls down his pants; then I tackle him with a desperate bear hug in an attempt to keep the rest of his clothes on. The doctor walks in and is startled by the WWF throw down going on. I laugh because I want to cry, and I try to explain, "He's fine, I swear. He just missed his nap today."

My daughter jumps up on the exam table as requested. Satan's little helper becomes obsessed with climbing on and jumping off of said table. I'm sweating from trying to keep the crazy one from leaping and hitting his face on the tile floor. All the while, the doctor is asking me about my five-year-old daughter's diet, and I'm telling her for the *fourth* year in a row, "She doesn't do well with vegetables."

I *again* pull my son off the table—then he performs his favorite new trick: spitting. The doctor,

I'm sure, is disgusted and my immediate thought is to swat my son's butt.

So now, not only am I paying half-ass attention to what the doctor is asking me, I nearly spank my child in front of her. She gives me a "don't spank" glare. Awkward.

The doctor continues her exam by looking in Big Sister's ears. Little Bothersome Brother is sitting quietly behind her on the exam table, but then he pushes her. The doctor damn near shoves the ear-light thingy into her skull, while giving me the dirtiest "can you *please* control your damn kid," look I've ever received. I want to die.

I apologize profusely and firmly plant the boy in a chair. I shove my cell phone into his tiny, two-year-old hands just as the doctor is informing me that at *five* years old, I should still be limiting my daughter's screen time.

The doctor leaves, and my daughter announces that she has to go to the bathroom. At this point, I would rather lick a germ-infested shape sorter than take the ticking-time-bomb boy out of this confined space. I tell her the bathroom is just down the hall and to go ahead without me, I'll be right in our doorway, and she'll see me as soon as she comes out.

Well, Raging Bull sees an open door and charges. I fly after him, but it's too late. He opens the door to the next exam room, where another doctor is seeing a patient. The doctor gasps, the boy laughs, and I cringe and apologize. I run with him back to our room and shut the door. The doctor from next door enters our room and "politely" asks me to keep my child in our assigned room. *Thanks, doc, I'll work on that. Oh, and did I mention, he didn't nap today?*

As I rest my head on the arm pressed against the door to keep my son from escaping again, I remember my daughter! I grab my boy and open the door. I walk out with a "where's my freakin' kid" look on my face, and the Little Man flails and screams while on my hip because I won't let him run. A staff member sees me and asks, "Are you the mother that lost her kid?" I fight the urge to spew sarcasm on the judgmental stranger "rescuing" my daughter. Apparently, while I was wrangling my boy from another patient's room, his sister got lost in a hallway. My bad.

The nurse finally shows up. I jokingly tell her to hurry and shoot up my daughter. (My parenting humor was lost on Nurse Ratchet's evil twin.) I hand my phone back to Little Man as he practically dry humps my leg in an attempt to be held.

Inoculation accomplished, I grab the monsters and head to check out. As I'm scheduling my daughter's next visit, I remind the kids they are allowed one sticker. The Little Turd and his sort-of-behaving sister start fighting over who has more stickers. I decline a reminder card and inform my children with my eyes that we are leaving *NOW!*

I grab my son by one hand and part walk, part pull him out of the office. His sister is whining because her brother's other hand is full of stickers; meanwhile, she only has six. With a total Momma-on-the-edge voice, I tell her life isn't fair. She decides not to push it.

I load the kids up in their car seats and vow to never, *ever* let naptime slide again. I throw the truck in reverse and look behind me just in time to see my baby boy closing his eyes. *Sleep, you sweet little monster, just sleep.*

Running on Empty

Jenny Kanevsky

"Running on Empty" is not just a great Jackson Browne song, it's a state of being in which, like many mothers, I find myself lately.

My family was slammed with back-to-back sicknesses including two rounds of strep, several colds, croup, and a trip to the ER. It was ten straight days of me caring for a sick child, a sick me, or both. And just when everyone was well, I got hit with one more three-day whammy of a cold-flu. And, as the stay-at-home mom in this scenario, the burden fell on my shoulders.

During all of this, I was a mess: One day I took the boys to the doctor while still in my pajamas. Another day I asked a drive-thru Starbucks barista how many packs of instant coffee came in a twelve-pack.

She did a double take.

I said, "Did I just ask you how many are in a twelve-pack?"

"Yes ma'am you did."

"Huh," I replied. "Feel free to tell whomever you want about this."

She smiled and said, "Ma'am, you made my day."

I needed a break: not just a few hours, but an overnight, maybe two, pampering, checking out—a mini "strike."

So tomorrow after dropping the kids at school, I will be off the clock for a few days. I am taking myself, a bottle of wine, books, DVDs, my cats (because relaxing, reading, and watching movies all day is just not the same without my cats), plus some snacks to the W Hotel for the weekend. Yes, the W. I am going to a hot-sh** hotel for two nights (buy one night, get one half off) and I can't wait.

I did something else after my meltdown. I confessed to my family that I felt taken advantage of and that I expected change. I reassured my boys that I loved them—I loved being their mom, and taking care of them was a job I relished. But I also wanted appreciation, respect, gratitude, "thank yous," and an awareness of the work that goes into maintaining a home, taking care of people, feeding, driving, and nursing someone back to health.

I also needed to know that they loved it too.

I wanted them to learn not just to appreciate me, but to appreciate their lives, what they had, how lucky they were. At the risk of using the "children are starving in Africa" defense, I told them, "We live in a community where everyone plays a part, everyone needs to be loved and appreciated, and not to run on empty."

Then I informed them I was going away for the weekend.

"Are you going because you're mad at us, Mom?" my older son asked.

"No sweetie. I'm not mad. But I do need a break, some time for myself where I don't have to take care of anyone but me. When I come back, I'll feel better."

My younger boy immediately hugged me, sat back down at the table, and said, "Thanks for the pasta, Mom."

And they acted better and more appreciative after our talk.

Maybe I didn't need to go away after all?

Nah, W Hotel, here I come!

Snooze Buttons and No-Sleep Fairies

Michelle Matthews

I have a fairy that lives in my house. I call her the No-Sleep Fairy. Some nights I imagine her standing over my bed looking down at me with a taunting look in her eye. I want to smack that expression off her face and go to sleep.

She has minions. They hide in plain sight disguised as my children, the dog, and my husband—and they are all hell bent on not letting me get to sleep. There are seven of us in my family: a set of tweens, a random kindergartener, and a set of toddlers thrown in just for the fun of it. The No-Sleep Fairy works her strongest magic through the *littlest people* in the house and those *two-year-olds* take no prisoners.

Now that I'm a mom I never have enough time for sleep, and sleep doesn't have time for me. Just when I think I can catch up and feel like a normal human being, something happens: an illness sweeps through the house or there's a change in someone's schedule. But losing sleep is always the bottom line. No matter how much Mr. Sandman tries to find me, that damn No-Sleep Fairy is bound and determined to have her greedy little way.

It starts after I put my book on the nightstand (a book I've been trying to read since I had the second child).

I can hear the noise from the radio blaring out of one of the tween's rooms. The toddlers are going to hear it too. Any minute now they are going to wake up and think that it's play time. So I roll out of bed and make my way downstairs to the tween cave. I go through the motions of telling him to turn it down, followed by *no that's not low enough* before making my way back to the bedroom. I get into bed, finally relaxed again, and then I hear fussing from the girls' room. *You have to be kidding me!*

I'm not the only one who hears this—I can't be. But there's my husband, splayed out on his stomach, dead asleep. I can't blame him for all of my sleep problems. He could sleep through World War Three and the Zombie Apocalypse simultaneously raging outside his window.

I stomp down the hall to the girls' room and diffuse another "end of the world" situation. Tonight's installment of "she has my stuffed bear" is sorted out, and everyone is kissed and tucked away in bed again.

At this point I have to be stealthy. I'm dangerously close to the toddler bedroom, and if one twin should so much as sniff out my presence there will be crying. I try my best to tiptoe down the hall with moves akin to a ninja assassin, but I'm caught. I can hear the cries of "Momma" on the other side of the door. I have to go in and put out the toddler bomb before it explodes into full-on meltdown. I go in, lie down, and fall asleep in my son's bed only to wake up at midnight on the floor after being kicked out.

Finally, I'm back in my own bed. My husband rolls over and, with his extraordinary sleep strength, pins me down in the most uncomfortable position. I lie there staring at the ceiling unable to move and whisper, "I could totally fall asleep like this and wake up with a sore neck." I decide to shove him aside and make myself comfortable.

Soon I feel myself drifting off, but that dang blasted fairy isn't done with me yet. She sets the dog on me. The long slurping noises that he makes cause my eyes to twitch. His slurps are only matched by my husband's snoring, which can go from a low rumble to a mighty lion roar, and each time I try to shift to get more comfortable he snores louder.

Instead of counting sheep I count zombies eating sheep. I try to imagine my neighbors as zombies, but stop short as I plan out my day. I write parts of my novel in my head and plan my blog entry while my husband sleeps peacefully—it makes the insomniac in me jealous.

While he's lying there curled up beside me like a cherub, I'm steaming. I hear him breathing in my ear. I will not go back to sleep anytime soon.

Finally I resign. I wave the white flag and the fairy zips away only to come back when my husband's alarm goes off at 5:30. It is set to the sound of a waterfall with music—it's supposed to be very soothing and relaxing but to me the noise is like an air-raid siren and jolts me awake.

Once I hear the alarm I'm pissed because *he's* not getting up. *Why would you set it and not get out of bed when it goes off?* (I've been asking myself that question for years.) He will hit the snooze button every five minutes from now until he decides to get up, and I will hear the air-raid siren over and over again.

He should be able to feel the death glare I'm giving him in the darkness as he leans over and smacks the snooze button. Finally sleep finds me and I'm back to counting zombies eating sheep. I let my mind travel to images of World War Z in which a zombie horde would not eat me—I'm too sleep deprived and sickly— they would eat all the healthy people in the house first. At least then I would finally get some rest.

First Fight

Tina Parker

It was naptime
You told me poo poo
and ran

I caught you
          I held your arms
You twisted
until you went red

Your eyes bulged
          you went boneless

I needed rest
But you would not   stop

I closed the door
To keep you in there

Tina Parker

You banged
and shouted   Mama
                    Mama come in here

I swung the door in
fast
and caught your toe

I offered to kiss your boo-boo
I tried to rock you
                    No way Mama   go away
                    Mama

You shooed me
with your hand
You'd not take

my lap
or your bed

you slept   belly down   bare legs

on the cold
wood floor

The Five Stages of Exhausted Cooking

Mary Widdicks

I have two kids under the age of four and a Netflix subscription, which means I never sleep past 7:00 a.m., and I can't go to bed without watching just one more episode of *House of Cards*. I'd say my sleepiness ranges from "Yeah, I could use a nap" to "Crap, what time is it and where is the baby?" The bags under my eyes are a good indication of my level of exhaustion and my energy level, but you can also tell how much sleep I've had by the type of breakfast I serve my children.

Here is my handy little reference chart (in case you stay the night and are too frightened to ask me how my night went, which in the later stages of exhaustion, is a valid fear).

Stage Zero: When I'm fully rested and excited to greet the new day, I will serve my children perfectly round golden blueberry pancakes with fresh-squeezed orange juice, farm-fresh uncured bacon, and scrambled eggs. (I'll let you know if that ever happens.)

Stage One: "Yeah, I could probably use a nap." This is a very optimistic, six-to-eight hours of solid, unbroken, no one pees in their bed, no one's sucking on my boobs while I sleep, kind of rest. On the rare occasion I find myself in this nirvana-like state—my birthday, holidays, *my-husband-wants-something* days—I like to rustle up my signature pancakes. (Okay, I like to pour some Bisquick into a bowl and add milk. But still. It's freaking pancakes.) Unfortunately there's a 50/50 chance one side will burn while I'm shoveling yogurt into the baby's mouth between flippings. I figure syrup hides all manner of sins. Throw a few chocolate chips on there and my kids would eat a shoe.

Stage Two: "I can't keep my eyes open." Stage two is my baseline. It means I spent six-to-eight hours in bed, but I was up for one reason or another at least twice in the night.

My family calls this stage "sleep dominos" just to torture me. It's when one member of the family wakes me up by either peeing himself in bed, peeing loudly in the toilet, or jumping on my head. Then another child wakes up and wants milk or the dog pees on the leg of the bed or poops in the closet, and

The Five Stages of Exhausted Cooking

I wake up my husband with my scrubbing and he needs to pee. (Are you following me?)

On these mornings, I muster up the energy to pour some cheerios into a bowl with cut-up bananas, milk, and a glass of juice. I then sit at the table with the three-year-old and check my email while he eats and the baby picks at Cheerios in his high chair. It may not be the ideal family breakfast but it's calm and quiet.

Stage Three is a common occurrence in our house these days, days when I've been staring at *Thomas the Train* for fifteen minutes without blinking. My brain shuts down and turns on some much-needed auxiliary power. It's not quite a crisis. These are the days when I've had four to five hours of interrupted sleep, and I start to feel like a fired extra from *The Walking Dead.* On these mornings I tell the three-year-old he can have anything that he wants for breakfast as long as it can be heated in the micro-wave or toaster: Eggos, pizza, hot dogs, pop tarts—and if it doesn't have to be heated, he can chase it with some chocolate milk. One time he ate cold spa-ghetti and he loved it.

Stage Four: I shut my eyes for a few minutes while my kid is on the toilet. At this stage I've had a few hours of sleep and I'm achy—spending a few hours in bed can cause my back and neck to ache as if I woke up from a week-long coma. On these mornings it's less about nutrition and more about survival. We head over to the living room where I hand the three-year-old a baggie of dry cereal and a sippy cup of milk, turn on the TV, and let Mickey Mouse babysit my kid while I search the house for anything caffeinated that is not moldy.

Stage Five: "Crap, what time is it and where is the baby?" On days like this no one is eating breakfast until I've had at least 500 mg of caffeine. (If there's food on the floor and it's edible, go for it.)

I've reached Stage Five only a couple of times, usually when I've been ill and either pregnant or with a newborn, but so far no one has suffered any permanent scarring. (However, if you suspect that I might be approaching a Stage Five exhaustion emergency, it might be wise to give me some extra space. It's a tossup whether or not I'll bite your nose off, burst into tears, or collapse into a narcoleptic coma. In any case run—run far, far away.)

Jet Lag: The Torture Chamber

Lisa Webb

I am passed out on the bed, unable to get up, while my poor, confused toddler is poking at me, pulling my arm, pleading with me to get up. I did not take any drugs or have any alcohol. It's the middle of the night and I just flew over the Atlantic Ocean and across Canada with two children under the age of three.

My two-year-old is telling me to get up because she thinks it's time for Cheerios, but my body is stuck to the mattress as if I've been super-glued to the sheets.

There's no way I can get up. I tell her I just need a minute to rest my eyes. I slip into thirty-eight seconds of heavenly deep sleep until her pointer finger taps on my forehead over and over again while she sings "Forehead, forehead, forehead."

The tapping teleports me back to my adolescence when my older brother would pin me down, tap on my forehead the same way, telling me to "name 20 cereals" and keep up the forehead banging until I rattled off every cereal that my teenage brain could come up with. Both were equally tortuous.

After a couple hours of rocking, singing, humming, and begging her to sleep, I slip in and out of consciousness. My toddler's eyelids finally close, and mine come crashing down like the curtain on the final scene of a dramatic play.

Twenty minutes of the deepest sleep of my life, and then I hear my six-month-old screaming for her turn to get up. Back to pulling my body from the sheets and willing my limbs to wake up so I can pick up my baby.

With my husband back home in France, I'm temporarily a single Mom who is dealing with an eight-hour time change and two nocturnal babies who take turns testing the limitations of my sanity.

We're back in Canada visiting my parents, who are trying to help, but instead they are spoiling my daughters during the day while I ping-pong between them at night.

Jet Lag: The Torture Chamber

I long for my husband, and I can't wait to see him again. I miss being able to elbow him and say, "Your turn." I dream of his muscular arms wrapped around our daughters while I sleep for hours, recovering from the exhaustion of sleepless nights and days that start at 3:00 a. m.

When our days and nights return to normal, there's only a small window of time before we return home to France and do it all over again.

I'm putting this in writing because I seem to have amnesia when it comes to traveling overseas with just our children.

Sleep has become a lover that my travel-tired body can't get enough of. It's like a drug, and I am going through some serious withdrawal. So if you're getting some shut-eye tonight, sweet dreams my friends. Maybe I'll join you again one day. Until then, pass the coffee.

Insomnia Is Nothing to Lose Sleep Over

Sarah Almond

I'm a half-sleeper: I stay up until midnight and I don't sleep as long as I should. Once the sun is up, it's a crapshoot as to how long I'll snooze. (I suffer from a form of insomnia called "I drink too much caffeine during the day and worry too much at night.")

There are a few external causes including 1) my eight-year-old daughter, otherwise known as The Princess, 2) my husband the Klingon, and 3) my eight-year-old son, The Professor.

The Princess is a morning person. She wakes up early, jumps out of bed, and is happy about it, regardless of what time she went to bed the night before. She inherited this *annoying trait* from my father. He used to rise with the sun and sing to my mother. (Somehow she let him live.)

My husband is just the opposite. He takes the prize for morning grouchiness. I won't speak to him in the morning if it's before ten in the morning (lest I lose a body part). I've made the mistake of trying to communicate with him as early as eight.

Me: "Have you seen my phone?"

Husband: "RAAAAAAAAAHR!"

His grumpiness is advantageous on the weekends because I get to sleep in late: The Princess will peek into the bedroom, see Daddy's sleeping form, and retreat back to her bedroom.

My eight-year-old son is disagreeable most mornings. He uses so much brainpower during the day that he requires large quantities of sleep. Heaven forbid if I let him sleep in, but heaven forbid if I wake him up. On Saturdays he sleeps in, and I check in on him periodically. When I go back in at nine he's often still asleep. At 9:05 he yells at me from the bedroom, so I enter his room to see what he wants.

The Professor: "Why didn't you wake me up? I've been waiting and waiting for you to come get me!"

The next day I wake him up at 8:00 a.m. (because, after all, he yelled at me the morning before).

The Professor: "Why are you waking me up? I want to sleep in!"

I can't win.

This is when I go back to sleep on the couch (and because I was up until 2:00 a.m.).

Most days I stay up half the night so I can be tired all day. I call it "The Insomnia Show." I watch infomercials on TV. (I really could use that Perfect Pancake Maker.) Or I go on the Internet and look up all the symptoms I imagine I'm having. For example, I have a zit on my neck and according to Google it's cancer; or my neck hurts, so it must be meningitis. If I have a headache, it must be a tumor.

I take half an Ambien pill at night to sleep. When I do fall asleep, it's only for a few minutes. If I take the other half, I'm still up.

I've tried other remedies: drinking soothing, lemon verbena tea; taking valerian root or melatonin; and my personal favorite—wine. Sometimes I turn on my noise machine and listen to it play rain sounds as I burn cedar or lavender incense. (Maybe someday I will ask my grouchy-in-the-morning hubby for a nighttime massage.)

Why don't I sleep? It is a combination of ADD and anxiety. I lie awake and think random, anxious thoughts for hours without interruption. (My brain welcomes the opportunity and runs with it.)

When I do go to bed without assistance from a foreign substance, I experience a weird, *half-awake, half- asleep thing*: I'm in my bed, I'm dreaming, but I'm not fully asleep.

During the day I could go-go-go nonstop (and pray I'm tired enough to sleep through the night). Or I could take an antihistamine or a Xanax and sleep for days. (And as wonderful as that sounds, three people would be upset with me.)

But whom am I kidding? I will continue to wander the Internet until the wee hours of the morning; or surf infomercials on TV (while my kitchen fills up with nifty gadgets).

Ah, to sleep—perchance even to dream, throughout the night. Someday, I'll be a whole-sleeper.

Many a Sleep Between the Cup and the Lip

Devyani Borade

My bedside clock shrills and haughtily announces the time: five a.m. My hand strikes like a snake and strangles off the alarm, mid-scream. I glance nervously at the two sleeping forms by my bedside. The larger of them stirs, licks her lips, and turns over, noisily twisting her sheets around her three-year-old frame tighter than a lock of hair caught in a bad perm. The other continues sleeping. *Phew.*

Putting aside all murderous thoughts about the insane person who invented the alarm clock to keep mothers like me forever on the edge, I get out of bed, navigate to the washbasin, and fumble to turn on the tap. The stream of water is so icy cold that it numbs my hands. I muster enough courage to sprinkle some on my face. Each drop feels like the quill of a porcupine as it hits my eyes and stings them open.

I stare at my reflection in the mirror: a face that would have launched a thousand face creams.

The toothpaste squishes out of the tube as if under duress. Then it performs its dirty work without fuss and makes a determined attempt to sweep out the remaining vestiges of last night's dinner from between stubbornly misaligned teeth.

My eyes, espying their opportunity, begin to close again. My nose twitches and begins to run. The towel looks on as if with distaste as my hand reaches for it and forces it to wipe my face.

I move toward a part of the house that was demarcated a gymnasium when I was in a mad fit of health consciousness. *Must get fit. Must get my pre-pregnancy body back.* Those are the thoughts in my heart. My head, on the other hand, reminds me that I have a shape like an hourglass figure lying on its side.

My home "gym" is a meter square of open space in the middle of the spare bedroom, with a mat spread on the floor. Visions of me curled up snugly and snoring swim in front of my eyes.

Resolute, I push them away. *That mat is for exercising the body, not resting it,* I say sternly to myself as I step on the mat.

Then visions of gorgeous supermodels, like Naomi and Cindy, with perfectly toned muscles and curves, begin to take shape, with "a perfect me" posing alongside them and flashbulbs popping all around.

Many a Sleep Between The Cup and The Lip

Then I realize it isn't paparazzi cameras flashing; it's the overhead light bulb that my husband just switched on. He's come to see why I am making a perfect fool of myself earlier than usual this morning.

"Oh, you're exercising," he states as he rolls his eyes, shrugs, and returns to his warm side of the bed.

For a moment, I look on, envious, then steel my resolve and return my gaze to the mat. As if on cue, new visions appear. This time it's me puffing and panting with dumbbells, breaking out in a sweat. I sigh. I must've been drunk when I decided to exercise at 5:30 a.m. (or my brains must be pickled in the heat).

My resolve begins to melt as I look at myself in the mirror again. Lo! What is this I see? I am not so fat! Plump perhaps, chubby even, but with proper care while dressing, and a longish stretch of imagination, I might even pass for a *comfortable* mum, whose love handles exist solely for her little cherubs to grab onto to keep their noggins from cracking when they slip off the sofa or vault off the breakfast table.

What are a few fat cells? It's what is in the mind, heart, and soul that matters, and I'm not doing too badly. A huge load lifts from my mind. I smile. The body beautiful can wait. I am going back to sleep.

Depression, I Hate You

Sara Green

My sole identity has become *all things Mom* after having kids. I've been striving to become the person I was *before* kids and remain a kick-ass mom.

There are days when I struggle to get out of bed and days when I can't seem to sit still, but the difficult part: depression. I'm learning to not let it control me and my ongoing battle is kicking depression's sorry ass out the door. It's hard because my motivation is exhausted: the energy I have goes directly to entertaining and caring for my boys, who are five and two.

The other day my toddler became Godzilla and poured a box of Q-tips on the bathroom floor and destroyed our "marble museum." This prompted my oldest to sigh and say, "He's at it again."

My boys will bicker over toys and then won't accept a solution from the "mean mommy monster." Later, a game of hide 'n' seek will be played. They'll take turns hiding and seeking. The toddler will proudly count in gibberish, which the oldest translates as if he were fluent in "the tongue of the toddler."

Lunch time starts out bumpy. Little tummies growl while eyes and hands are on the prowl. Quickly, I dash to heat up pasta with marinara and spinach. The ding of the plates hits the table (a call to be seated) and the trotting of fast feet is heard. However, disappointment fills their eyes. *Ah, it's going to be one of those battles.* Sorrow-filled cries call out, "This doesn't look yummy. I don't like pasta. There is something green in here." But, before the plates are pushed away in disgust, the mean mommy monster appears with magical mozzarella cheese that they happily sprinkle on their pasta. It's nice to hear silence when they devour their meal.

It's ridiculously hard, but I push through the day *for them*. However, I want to lie down and sleep, sleep, sleep, and sleep some more. This need to rest tugs at me all day. I want to shove the pressure away and accomplish something, anything, like mopping the floor or going to the store and buying milk. (Is it sad that those small moments feel like big accomplishments?)

It's not that I'm scared, necessarily, but stuck. My mind is in overdrive, listing tasks and activities that I need or want to do. But physically, I can't move.

How do I fix this? I have to get up, get out, and simply do what comes to mind. Yet, I'm bound by an invisible rope. I'm tugging and tugging hard. I know that with each tug the rope is loosening. It's a struggle and I cannot give up. It's a phase I've battled many times before and conquered; and my negative thoughts will bind that rope tighter: *Why can't I do this simple task? Why is it so easy to give up? Why do I have depression?*

I can't hate myself for this disease. I have to acknowledge it and work hard at moving it out of my life and stop comparing myself to others. I can't help that my day isn't full of activities, social dates, get-togethers, and adventure or that there isn't much to do outside of keeping up with the house and raising my boys. Wait! Did I just say life isn't much outside of raising my boys? That's plenty of life, and I have to remember that. We might not have money to go to the zoo or the museum this week, but there is a world of adventure as soon as we walk outside. It's okay that my life is simple. It can be great with each moment with my kids, even if it's just reading a book or putting a puzzle together. I have to remember that. *It's okay. It will be okay.*

Parental Paralysis

Stephanie Sprenger

There's a good reason sleep deprivation is used as a form of torture: not sleeping one night here or there isn't pleasant, but night after night for months on end is downright agony. After surviving fifteen months of frequent night awakenings, I now consider myself to be a sleep-deprivation veteran, a classification worthy of a bumper sticker, signature tattoo, secret handshake, or possibly even a parade. I have emerged from the fog; I feel like a hero (albeit one with fewer brain cells, a tendency to leave my grocery list at home, and more disjointed conversational patterns). I suffered from a variety of symptoms of long-term sleep deprivation, not the least of which I call Parental Paralysis.

After my oldest daughter was born I'd had a few rough nights but I never succumbed to the glassy-eyed hazing of many of my fellow moms. When she was five years old, her baby sister, Sophie, was born. At first she had me fooled; Sophie slept well at night and took solid daytime naps. I mistakenly congratulated myself for having won the baby jackpot again. Within a matter of weeks, however, she began to turn on me.

My clever daughter decided to use Mommy as her personal all-night snack machine, nursing every few hours, often enough to sufficiently disrupt my sleep cycle. I found countless excuses: teething, colds, and traveling, but it came down to that blasted parental curse—The Path of Least Resistance. And it won every time.

My fragmented sleep cycles during those dark months left me cloudy. I became groggy and grumpy, disorganized, irritable with my older daughter, and a spacey, uninspired conversationalist. (This caused me to fantasize about the next morning's coffee at 4:30 in the afternoon.)

I discovered that the most problematic side effect of this long-term sleep deprivation wasn't tiredness, it was Parental Paralysis. It rendered me incapable of completing items on my to-do list, planning fun enrichment activities for my family, deciding on an appropriate restaurant or take-out menu for dinner (because cooking regularly was laughable), and generally maintaining an organized, non-disgusting household.

When both girls *finally* fell asleep for the night (for a few hours, more likely), I wanted to tidy up the family room, wipe down the kitchen counters, and put away some laundry, because I knew it would make me feel better in the morning. Instead, I slumped uselessly on the couch, engaging in confrontational fantasies and mentally drafting strongly worded letters to various hypothetical tyrants while eating ice cream with a glazed expression on my face.

One such evening, my husband and I were stretched out in front of the television, and I commented to him that we should bring up the one-year-old clothes from storage.

"Mm-hmm," he grunted in response.

"Should we also re-implement Izzy's behavior reward system? And start doing her brain balance exercises?" I continued sleepily.

"Yep," he confirmed unenthusiastically.

"How about we revise our budget, sort through the bag of crap, and act like better humans?" I continued.

I had become paralyzed: Parental Paralysis was preventing me from engaging in an array of household tasks. Not to be deterred, I made a list.

Promptly clip the fingernails and toenails of my children. (Or, shudder—myself.)

Offer a balanced and diverse selection of after-noon snacks.

Prepare meals (meals that involve more than a pot and one wooden spoon).

Plan ahead for future travel. (Did I *really* want to take my kids anywhere? I hated taking them with me to the *grocery store*.)

Frame and hang photos taken in the recent past. (My second child had no hope of making it to the living room wall.)

Organize and complete my baby book. (Stop laughing.)

Mail thank-you cards, holiday letters, and party invitations (in a timely manner).

Keep on top of socially acceptable hygiene practices: regular showers, haircuts, and dental care. (Pedicures and waxes were entirely out of the question.)

One day my husband and I were finally shamed into cleaning out our van: our friend's daughter commented that it was "too crowded" in our car. We had taken her to school, and she had to step carefully over mounds of crushed goldfish crackers, discarded Happy Meal contents, stuffed animals, and forgotten footwear, on her way to the back seat. The meaning of her observation was clear: it was five-year-old speak for, "Lady, you have too much crap in your car."

Unless I was being humiliated by the peers of my children, I just could not make the household run smoothly.

Even though I am a safe distance from those exhaustion-riddled months, my practices haven't evolved much and the sleep deprivation that caused my Parental Paralysis has given way to the Toddler Tornado. I shrug my shoulders and repeat my motto: "Why do I even bother?" about everything from sweeping the kitchen floor to organizing the Tupperware cabinets. Maybe one day I'll resume the practices of my pre-child years, like taking pride in the appearance of our home, resuming an efficiently operating household, and becoming organized. I guess I can look forward to that fleeting window of time between the onset of Empty Nest Syndrome and full-blown senility.

Top 10 Ways NOT to Fall Asleep

Lucia Paul

Number One: Lie awake thinking about various fears, and then realize that narcissism is in fact all about focusing on you. Factor in that narcissism can dwell side-by-side with being a sociopath. If you have a teenager, you can be certain he or she is a sociopath along about 3:00 a.m.

Number Two: Speaking of 3:00 a.m., I sincerely hope you have not seen the movie *The Exorcism of Emily Rose*. Now that I have brought it up, it's a fantastic way to not fall asleep. Once you've seen it, you will become acquainted with the idea that 3:00 a.m. is "The Time of The Devil." (After seeing the movie, I woke up for months at exactly 3:00 a.m. Don't worry because this will happen to you too.)

Number Three: Ask yourself, "Is there a sex tape of me somewhere, anywhere? What if that one guy in college secretly made one and all parents at my children's school have seen it?" Not a wink will you see!

Number Four: Realize you have a vague leg pain. Further realize that the articles you have read about various diseases clearly highlighted *Vague Leg Pain* as a precursor to certain death.

Number Five: Do the math of figuring out how much you will need to live from retirement age (don't forget inflation) until your death—if vague leg pain doesn't kill you first. With the way medical advances are going, that's about 42 years. Good luck sleeping!

Number Six: Take an over-the-counter sleeping pill, and then wonder if buying generic vs. name brand affects the strength. Fight sleep to the death as you become certain that generic is inferior.

Number Seven: Recall that Elvis liked to sleep in a freezing-cold room. In fact, all famous sleepers deeply enjoyed a frigid and tomb-like sleep environment. Fume about the body heat your significant other is throwing off. Become obsessed with buying a "cooling" pillow the next day at Target.

Number Eight: Try to employ a "counting backwards" or a "count your blessings" tactic as a way of inviting sleep. Realize that, like a sobriety test, counting backwards is sort of hard. Count blessings, but then begin to veer off in other directions, such as

"I am so blessed to own a home. But the roof is super old. It will cost at least 20K to repair it. Where will we get 20K?"

Number Nine: Brainstorm about who would be cast as you in the movie of your life: Valerie Bertinelli? Not quite right. Sally Field? Too old. Miranda Kerr? Now we're talking. Move on to all family members and neighbors.

Number Ten: Obsess about all the people in your life who, no doubt, fall asleep with ease. Why them? Why not you? You're perfectly calm and rational.

Because falling asleep is so hard.

The Accidental Co-Sleeper

Melissa Swedoski

Ah, yes, bedtime. That magical time when I can drift off to sleep and dream of faraway lands and crazy adventures that let me be the leader of my own kingdom, beloved by all, adored by strangers (unless you have toddlers, which I do). Then it's a journey into finding out just how many ways I can contort my body to fit the one-foot wide sleeping space allotted by the world's tiniest bed hogs. Yes, I have become the accidental co-sleeper.

When we started this parenting journey, we never actively set out to be co-sleepers. My husband and I were perfectly happy to drift off to dream in our queen-size bed, each comfortable with plenty of room to sleep in any position we desired.

When we were still working, we never had our daughter, Annie, in the bed with us. If she woke up during the night I took her to the living room where we stayed until she went back to sleep. I returned her to her crib and left to go to the comfort of my quilted cocoon.

But then we moved in with my dad. Since space was at a premium, Annie's bed, rather her play yard, was at the foot of ours. I can remember nights hearing her cry and looking at the foot of the bed to see her tiny little head peeking at me. It was just easier to put her in the bed with us.

When we finally moved into our current home, she loved her room and slept through the night. When Leelou came along, she stayed in the play yard next to our bed, so if she woke, I could pick her up, soothe her a little, and put her back.

But a funny thing happened as they got older: they transitioned to beds on their own. However, once Annie transitioned to her toddler bed, she became quite adept at getting up, walking down the hall to our room, opening the door, and coming right on in.

I lost count of how many times I was awakened by, "Mommy?" in the tiniest little whispered voice. Sometimes I didn't hear her. I just sensed her staring at me. And it usually scared the crap out of me.

When Leelou moved into her own room, she sometimes woke up, and I would just crash with her in our guest bed. Then I would hear Annie crying for me, wandering around the hall, and waking everyone. I gave up staying in Leelou's room.

At some point, with one squirmy baby and one bed-hog toddler, we decided a queen size bed wasn't cutting it anymore. We supersized to king, and it initially seemed huge—plenty of room for everyone. But another funny thing happened: our daughters grew.

Generally, Leelou sleeps through the night, opting to stay in her own comfy space. She is a hard sleeper and usually doesn't want to get up in the morning. Annie, since potty training started, gets up every single night. At first, it was just to go to the bathroom, but now I don't know why—although she has repeatedly commented that she likes our bed better: yeah, me too.

We get lucky sometimes and have a two-night streak where they both stay ensconced in their beds. It's pure bliss when I wake up and realize that I have not had to hang on to the side of the bed like a drowning man clinging to a life raft. I actually have the room to stretch all the way out and allow my limbs to relax.

But there are mornings, like yesterday, when I woke to find Annie curled snugly against my leg, head at my feet, sleeping soundly. I have absolutely no idea how she got in the bed. Sure, I could have returned her to her bed, but that would've entailed getting up and mama ain't having it.

Perhaps if we'd planned better or discussed how we would handle what to do when our babies woke up in the night, I might not be the accidental co-sleeper. But, I wouldn't have received deliriously delicious cuddle time; or heard the giggles of my girls as they woke; or watched them sleeping on their daddy's chest.

Eh. I'll sleep on my own later. You know, after they have kids of their own.

A Tired Mommy's Prayer for Sleep

Tina Bietler

The dinner dishes are cleared and the dishwasher is humming. Homework is completed and the children are playing. I look at the clock that hangs on the wall. It is 6:00 p.m. Only two hours until the children go to bed and I can have some peace and quiet; a small window of time for a hard-working, tired mommy to sit on the sofa and fold the basket of laundry while catching a few minutes of *Supernatural* on TV. *Damn, that <u>Jensen Ackles</u> is a hubba hubba!*

The clock continues to tick by. I count down the minutes until I can rest my exhausted head on my squishy, soft pillow. "Dear Lord, let them sleep, please Lord let ME sleep," I whisper under my breath.

The laundry is folded and put away, the last pile of papers has been graded and shoved back into my school bag, and the preview for next week's episode

Tina Bietler

of *Supernatural* is over (thank God). It is finally time for bed.

I slip between my sheets and let out a sigh. I hope I don't have to pee. I didn't have anything to drink after dinner just to make sure. (And I hope my husband isn't in the mood because I am too tired.)

After kissing the hubby goodnight, I roll over and close my eyes. Suddenly I remember that tomorrow we are starting the Science Unit on plants and I forgot to make the student response journals. I'll have to do that as soon as I get there in the morning. Oh, and I need to sign the permission slip for my twelve-year-old, AJ. I should have done that tonight. Soon, exhaustion quiets my overactive mommy brain, and around ten-thirty, sleep finally arrives.

Casey, my five-year-old, enters the room at eleven o'clock. He says he is thirsty, his throat is dry, and he needs water *now*. I take him into the kitchen and give him a tiny bit. He downs it and asks for more. I give him a second cup and then escort him back to bed, tuck him in, and give him another kiss goodnight.

Luckily it is still early. (I have time for tons of sleep, right?)

Warm and cozy, not wanting to get up, my bladder wakes me and demands attention. (Ever since the second baby, not only do I cross my legs to cough and sneeze, I pee every hour during the day and at least once during the night.) I climb out of bed, run to the bathroom, and then hurry back. I know I shouldn't, but I look at the clock. It is 1:32 a.m. If I fall asleep right away I should be able to get three-and-a-half more hours of sleep.

I lie there and lie there and lie there some more. I am still awake when AJ gets up to use the bathroom at 2:24. "BAM!" Surprise, he slammed the toilet seat again. At least he remembered to flush. *Okay Lord, if you let me fall asleep right now, I will still be able to get two- and-a-half hours. Please, I really need some sleep.*

Miraculously I nod off, but then wake with a start. Something is wrong. Crying? Oh, Casey is crying. I hop out of bed and find Casey running back and forth in the living room doing a sleepwalk version of the potty dance. I grab him because I know he is going to pee any second, but because he is still asleep he can't find the bathroom. We run to the bathroom and I yank his pajama bottoms down to his ankles and position him in front of the toilet. He all but sighs with relief as he answers the call of nature. For the second time in one night, I take him back to his room. I toss a blanket over him and skip giving him another kiss. I am just too tired and besides, he is already asleep. I go in my room and notice that it is 3:15 a.m.

"God, when I said I needed sleep I meant more than twenty minutes worth," I grumble. Apparently one should not grumble at God. He has a way of getting the last laugh. Five minutes later my husband begins to snore, quietly at first, which I try to ignore, but soon the whole room is rumbling with his inhales and exhales. Resisting the urge to smother him with a blanket, I elbow him in the side and he rolls over.

God, if you let me fall asleep now, I can still get ninety minutes of real sleep, please. You know, that stuff they call REM. Pretty please!

I lie there for a while, hoping to nod off soon, and I think I am just about to when suddenly Bella, the cat, begins to cry for food and affection. I try desperately to ignore her. She knows I am ignoring her, so Bella starts to paw at the door. *Scrape, scrape, meow. Scrape, scrape, meow.*

I get out of bed, grab a pillow, and throw it out the door at the cat. It is 4:30 in the freaking morning. Now when I climb back into bed I am angry. So angry in fact that sleep is out of the question. I begin to think about all the stuff I have to do today: run off those science papers, get the new grades into the computer, run to the market after work, and cook a super fast dinner because Casey has Cub Scouts.

A Tired Mommy's Prayer for Sleep

The alarm clock goes off at five sharp. I hit the clock a little harder than necessary and let out a yawn. I look up at the ceiling and, before I get out of bed to go chug two bottles of 5-hour Energy, I decide to flip God a double middle finger. I know it is wrong, and I will ask for forgiveness later, but right now I am tired, cranky, and honestly, He had it coming.

Ten Reasons Sleepovers Suck: A Cautionary Tale

Kathryn Leehane

Your kids are getting older, and bedtime battles are a thing of the past (maybe). They go to bed willingly and actually sleep through the night (mostly). You're just starting to enjoy regular REM cycles and solid stretches of sleep and feel almost human again (barely).

And then you decide to screw it all up.

I'm talking about sleepovers.

Who the hell invented sleepovers? Parents can barely survive the night with their own kids; why should they take in more?

Nonetheless, let's say you are going to have a sleepover with four kids: a younger son, an older daughter, and two friends (even though something deep down is telling you that this is a terrible idea). The evening will start out great because you will serve pizza and ice cream—classic sleepover food.

All four kids will then spend the evening playing cards and Apples to Apples and watching *Frozen* (because that brand of torture never ends).

By 9:30 p.m. you will get them started on their bedtime routine (i.e., you will force them to floss and brush their teeth and change into clothes that aren't covered in chocolate sauce and ice cream).

By 10:00 p.m. the kids will be downstairs with their sleeping bags ready for a campout.

Ten Reasons Why the Night Will Go Horribly Wrong

Reason #1: At 11:00 p.m. when the sleepover kids are quiet, you and your husband will doze off quickly in your bed, thanks to all the wine you drank. But it will last a mere twenty-three minutes.

Reason #2: At 11:23 p.m. a muffled whisper will wake you up (muffled because you wear earplugs to bed because your husband snores like a lumberjack with a megaphone duct-taped to his mouth). The barely audible whisper will come from your son. He and his friend will be thirsty, and you will direct them back downstairs to get some water *because, duh.*

Reason #3: You will awaken again at 11:47 p.m. by the whines of your son standing next to your bed with his friend who's now too hot to sleep. You will leave the comfort of your bed to get a fan, bring it downstairs, and plug it in. Mind you, the family room will be a pleasant 65 degrees (and for some reason the boy's sleeping bag will be a high-performance version rated for Mount Everest). Having risen out of bed, you will find it more difficult to fall back asleep this time. Also, your husband's snoring will have reached a new decibel level. But it will be just after midnight, and you will be damn tired, so you will fall asleep again after about fifteen minutes.

Reason #4: At 12:43 a.m. you will be woken up again, this time by a finger repeatedly poking you in the back. The finger will belong to your daughter, who is now your son's friend's keeper because your son will have fallen asleep, but the friend will still be unable to sleep. Through clenched teeth, you will suggest warm milk (which he won't want) and that your daughter read the friend a book (which she'll begrudgingly do because she's a nicer person than you are).

Reason #5: You will be awakened at 1:12 a.m. by four peering eyes and the strained voice of your daughter, who will have just read several stories to the child who could not fall asleep. She will be at the end of her rope and will not appreciate the irony of a younger child keeping her up all night. You will run out of ideas.

Reason #6: You will get kicked out of your own bed in order to let the *still-awake at 1:30 a.m.* child (who can't fall asleep downstairs nor in your son's room) co-sleep in *your* bed, which might not be a bad thing because your husband's snoring vibrates the entire bed like a T-Rex trying to sneak up on Jeff Goldblum.

Reason #7: The child will fall asleep in 30 seconds, and you will be forced to sleep in your son's room in a tiny bed surrounded by a minefield of Legos and Hot Wheels vehicles. Under the superhero sheets, at long last, you will fall asleep. (For exactly twelve minutes.)

Reason #8: At 2:14 a.m. your son will wake up, change his mind about the group campout, and kick you out of his bed (a bed that smelled like sweaty socks and foul morning breath), and you will miss that bed.

Reason #9: You will end up sleeping in your daughter's pink princess canopy bed with matching blankets and so many stuffed animals you will end up with two feet of sleeping space. You will angrily toss and turn and yawn and sigh, trying to combat the fact that you are now overtired to the point of insomnia. You will get approximately two hours of

Ten Reasons Sleepovers Sucks: A Cautionary Tale

uninterrupted sleep before your damn alarm announces that it's time to make breakfast for the kids and a gallon of coffee for yourself.

Reason #10: Your husband will wake up with a small human sleeping next to him and then go downstairs and walk into the kitchen with a confused look on his face, like a person with a hangover trying to piece together the sketchy details from the previous night.

And the moral of the story: put off sleepovers as long as you can. Or, better yet, ban them altogether. Because, let's face it, nobody sleeps during a sleepover—*nobody.*

Our Time

Anna Catarina Gragert

I started a tradition with my daughter, Anna, that I am now regretting: staying up *way* past her bedtime. It began after the twins were born. Anna was trying her best, but I could tell that she missed being the only child in our house. She looked longingly at her new siblings' cribs as if they were the pedestal that she had once stood on. Then she'd take all of her toys and arrange them around the cribs as if she were creating a moat.

One night I noticed Anna standing in the hallway, watching me rock the twins to sleep. Her big brown eyes seemed mesmerized, yet sad. So, I came up with a plan (because no mother can resist big, sad, brown eyes so late at night). "Anna, after the twins fall asleep, how about we spend some time together?" I asked, knowing that she would jump at the opportunity for alone time.

"Oh, yes! That sounds like so much fun," she gushed back to me.

At around 8 p.m. the twins fell asleep in my arms—now covered in drool. I placed them in their cribs and walked into the living room.

Anna was sitting on our musty floral couch. It was weird seeing her on the couch, in her pajamas, so late at night.

We didn't say anything. We simply nodded to acknowledge our agreement.

Anna looked over her right shoulder and glanced back at the clock. She had always been a stickler for the rules, so she was probably worried about staying up past her bedtime.

At some point, I must have put Anna back in bed, tucking her purple comforter around her tiny body. I must have done so because I woke up in bed the next morning without remembering how I got there. Anna didn't seem to remember last night's events either. It was as if it were all a mirage, with the only sign of our staying up being the exhaustion that was mutually felt. Ah, yes, the unforeseen effects.

This went on for weeks. It all seemed like some weird dream. I don't remember what we watched, what we said, or what we did. I just remember Anna looking back at the ivy-patterned clock every five minutes or so.

We called our late-night evenings together "Our Time." It was like an evening holiday, a time that

Anna and I could look forward to after caring for the twins.

Looking back, there was one "Our Time" moment that I remember vividly. Thirty minutes in, Anna looked at me and said in a serious voice, "Mommy, you have to check on the twins."

"Why? What's wrong?"

"The Ghostbusters' ghost is going to kidnap the twins, just like he did with the baby on the ledge," She replied nervously.

"Anna, don't worry about it. The twins are perfectly safe in their cribs."

"How do you know that? How do you know that the ghost didn't stretch out his arm, open the window, reach into the room, and kidnap the twins? I think you have to go check on them."

"Why don't you check on them, if you're so worried?" I countered.

"Because you're their mom."

Couldn't argue with that one, so I ran in and out of the twins' room, constantly on the lookout for the infamous Ghostbusters' ghost.

Part of me died that night from *sheer tiredness,* and I had an inkling that "Our Time" was going to come to a close *very, very* soon (either that or there was going to be a house-wide ban on all movies involving ghosts and their busters).

To Life

Amy Denby

"Is the pain dull?" my husband asked, yawning into the darkness, his lion's roar illuminated by the white glow of an iPad held an inch above his nose.

"No," I replied. A similar light beckoned from my nightstand, a grainy image on a baby monitor showed two-year-old twins thankfully asleep. The cable box glared with its green blur of time, 4:22 a.m. It taunted me, and I lay there thinking, *this is not the way to ring in the Fourth of July.*

Mike read the next question from the WebMD quiz displaying on his screen. "Does it sting?"

"No."

"Does it throb?"

"No." I paused, squeezing my fist and releasing it.

"Do you feel electric shock going down your arm?"

"No."

Alas, the WebMD quiz could not help me, and I did not need the all-knowing Doctor Google to tell me what was wrong. In my mind it was simple: I was having a heart attack, or a stroke, or I contracted West Nile Virus from the damn mosquitoes in the backyard, or E. Coli from the literal crap all over the house (thanks to potty training, which is less training, more just pee and crap yourselves wherever you want).

Regardless, the clock was ticking and I needed to know: *What could I do to save my life?*

"I think it's a stinger," Mike continued, interrupting the death sentence in my mind. "Or your collar bone. Or you fractured a rib. Either way, you're ridiculous."

Was it *so* ridiculous that I was *exhausted* after a day home with my twins? That, come bedtime, when they were finally asleep in their bedroom, *sweet Lord hay-Zeus*, I jumped into bed, ecstatic to have no one calling my name? Punching me in the buttocks? Showing me a poop that looked like a Wolf Man? (Actually, that last one was pretty cool.)

What's ridiculous is jumping onto a soft, padded bed, injuring myself, and throbbing in pain.

This body is only thirty-four years old. (Thanks, years of pilates, yoga, and one-armed pushups in boot camp classes. OMG, if I attempted to do that today, I would surely land splat on my face and die from multiple head wounds.) *What happened to that incredibly fit and nimble girl?* Oh yeah, she's home with two kids all day—cooking, cleaning, washing clothes, trying to write, and shower "when she can," which is mom-speak for never. She can't even work out at night in the basement like she used to. By then, even her toothbrush feels like a dumbbell (until she takes a flying leap into bed and *weeee*).

The prospect of another diagnosis besides cardiac arrest intrigued me. "What's a stinger?" I asked, attempting to prop myself on my elbows but wincing in pain.

"It's a football injury. You could've done that or pinched a nerve. I don't know. You need rest."

"You're just saying that because you want to go back to sleep, Denby," I teased, calling my husband by our last name as I sometimes do. The clock flicked to 4:23 a. m.

I thought about driving myself to the emergency room, but something about the emergency room at this hour felt too C.S.I. Maybe I could suck this up for the next few hours and go to urgent care in the morning, if I'm still alive. Please, Lord, don't let this be a heart attack. I don't want to die!

"You're not having a heart attack, *are you?*" (Was my husband reading my spiraling thoughts and giving ole grand-lady paranoia here a jab?)

"HOW WOULD I KNOW!" I snapped.

"Babe, I'm *kidding*, you're not having a *heart attack*. You hurt yourself being an idiot and taking a flying leap onto the bed. Besides, a heart attack would be your left side."

"CAN YOU LOOK THAT UP AND CONFIRM THAT?"

"You would know if you were having a heart attack. You'd be sweating."

"I AM SWEATING!"

"Don't you think it's from the heating pad you have on?"

"WHAT IF IT'S A COINCIDENCE?"

"I'm going to bed."

"DON'T LEAVE ME, DENBY!"

He rolled over and fell asleep, a mound under the sheets. And I watched the clock turn five, then six.

Around 8:00 a.m. I got out of bed and logged onto my computer and searched "Doctor Google."

I feverishly typed in "chest pain and arm pain" then an article on WebMD titled "Are you headed for a heart attack?" came right up.

Oh crap.

I read that an early warning sign of a heart attack is being tired—I'M FRIGGIN' EXHAUSTED! SO TIRED I FEEL LIKE CRAP ALL THE TIME! Then I found this gem: "When a woman suffers a heart attack she is more likely than a man to die."

"Watch the kids, Denby, I'm going to the doctor!" I hollered as I ran out the door. I heard the pitter patter of two tiny feet gaining close behind. As I turned to shut the door, shooing away reaching fingers, I caught eyes with my husband who asked me in a serious tone, "Hey, if you're not having a heart attack, can we still have the Walsh's over for a BBQ? After all, it's the Fourth of July."

I didn't answer him and pulled the door with a slam.

On the drive to the urgent care center, I told myself to stay calm. Breathe. Focus on the road. Ask the doctor if it's okay to eat an egg sandwich if you have a fatal heart condition because you're friggin' starving.

By the time I arrived at the office, all of the Advil I'd overdosed on had kicked it. It was a miracle, I was saved. I felt as if I could do those one-armed pushups again, oh yeah, if it weren't for that multiple head wound thing.

The waiting room was packed with antsy children. I could feel their germs and the glare of one heavily tattooed guy whose jeans were so tight I wondered how he pulled them over his feet. I contemplated leaving, but figured while I was there I might as well get an accurate diagnosis. I sent the following text to my husband. "Hey. Think I'm okay.

If you dress the kids can you put them in red, white, and blue star bathing suits?"

After all, it *was* the Fourth of July.

"Hey, hi, how are you," I began with a smile as the nurse took my vitals and filled out my chart. "So, um, this morning WebMD told me I was having a heart attack and I was going to die, so I wanted to rule that out before I have people over in a few hours for a Fourth of July barbeque."

Straight faced, "Oookaaay," the polite man said with pinched eyebrows. "Excuse me." He left the room and came back with another assistant, meaning I'm pretty sure he went out there and said, *Oh, we got a live one in here.*

"Mrs. Denby, what can we do for you?" boomed the male assistant with a smile that reeked of over-compensation.

I grinned in return and gave my spiel.

"I think I'm fine. I'm okay. I actually just jumped into bed last night because I was so tired and excited to be going to sleep that I'm pretty sure I just pulled a muscle or something. I'm better now. I just wanted to rule out—you know—anything more serious."

"You said a heart attack?"

Blinks, stares, and crickets.

"Um, well . . ."

"Are you having chest pain?"

"No."

"Does this hurt?"

"No."

"Your blood pressure and vitals are fine," he said, turning his attention to his clipboard.

Blinks, stares, crickets, and tumbleweeds.

"Yeah, well, okay, great! So, I can go?"

"You should be examined by the doctor."

I wondered what type of doctor he meant.

With that, the doctor came in. The physician's assistant who'd examined me said the following, verbatim: "Dr. Matthew, this is Mrs. Denby. She was overly excited in bed last night and she may have pulled a chest muscle."

Overly excited in bed? Forget the heart attack, now I was sure to die of embarrassment.

Please don't write that down, I mentally implored Dr. Matthew with my bleary eyes. But it was too late.

So I *scribbled down* my story as a reminder to think calmly and take care of health by sleeping (and not misdiagnosing myself with life-threatening illnesses in the dark of night). And most importantly, as I did later on at the Fourth of July barbeque, toast to life at any chance I got.

It's Too Early

Desiree Roundtree

My wonderful child decided to get out of bed today at 5:25 a.m., a full two hours before she had to get ready for camp.

"Mommy! Daddy! I want my tablet!"

My daughter was no longer in her room. She was now in *our* room, making her way to my side of the bed.

5:27 a.m.: "Kaelyn, go back to bed," I grumbled. She walked away, shoulders slumped, dejected.

I sat up and explained to her that if she stayed awake, she'd be too tired for camp.

It was 5:35 a.m., and I already wanted to scream. *Sheesh.*

I closed my eyes and attempted to get another hour of sleep. It was nearly impossible, since I knew my daughter was lying awake in the other room, upset that I didn't give her the tablet. As soon as I drifted off, I heard "Mommy! Daddy!"

I turned to see my husband, who was now out of bed, preparing for an early shift at work; then we both said, "Yes, Kaelyn."

She burst into our room and pronounced, "I want to sleep in your bed with you." And up she climbed, without a yes or a nod of approval and took over my husband's side.

After he showered, my husband attempted to help me get our daughter dressed for camp because she couldn't stand up. Her legs were jelly and she was sighing and throwing her head back.

Finally, we got her dressed.

"What do you want for breakfast?" my husband asked.

She shrugged her arms in an exaggerated, dramatic gesture." I don't know," she replied.

"We have oatmeal, Gorilla Munch, Cheerios, toast—what do you want to try?"

"I don't know."

I attempted to go back to bed. Twenty minutes later my daughter came into my room, having finished eating. *Thank the Lord in Heaven for small miracles.*

Now she was waving her stuffed Tiana doll wildly. "Mommy, Mommy, I want Tiana's legs to go like this!" And she yanked the dolls legs straight.

It's Too Early

We had a conversation about Tiana and her rigid legs; all the while she attempted to stuff her doll in the air conditioner, and she asked me to cut Tiana's fingers off.

It was 7:15 a.m.

She walked into the living room to play "Johnny and the Sprites" on the computer. Again, she barreled down the hallway to my room. "Mommy, I want to send Leonardo a card."

Leonardo is one of her friends from the program she went to last year. For two years they shared a classroom, and I believe she learned how to be a friend there.

"Okay, what made you think of Leonardo?"

"Nothing, really. Actually I wanted to send him a card a long time ago."

"So why didn't you ask or tell me."

"MOMMY CAN WE SEND HIM A TEXT CARD. OR AN EMAIL CARD. OR A TEXT EMAIL CARD."

"I will reach out to his parents today to say hello."

It was 7:36 a.m.

Seventy-five minutes later, I dropped my daughter off at camp and walked her to her classroom; she reminded me to send the text card and to drink a lot of water.

She then told me to enjoy my massage today and to take care of myself. I told her to do the same.

And as I left her classroom she said, "Mommy braided my hair today; that is why we are late. She is the best. Not at braiding, but at everything else."

This is what I love at 8:55 a.m.

Sleep When Baby Sleeps

Tricia Stream

I fear the days of my mom naps are coming to an end—never mind my full-time job, my after-hours writing gig, and cleaning up area-rugs after our dog has eaten yet another illicit item from a growing list of work boots, baseball gloves, and a week's worth of bananas. My twin toddler boys, Search and Destroy, have transitioned from the safety (I mean the danger) of their cribs to big-boy beds. This eventual nap-killing decision was brought about one morning when my husband and I woke our little apocalyptic horsemen from their angelic slumber only to discover Destroy perfecting his pommel horse gymnastic routine upon the railing of his crib.

Jon: That's really impressive.

Me: I know! That takes a lot of upper body strength.

Jon: And flexibility. You couldn't do that.

Me: Nope. But I'm working on stretching.

Destroy: MOMMEE! WATCH!

Jon: He's going to fall and break his neck.

Me: Probably.

Jon: I'll transform the cribs to toddler beds today.

We decided to introduce the boys to their new beds when they got home from school. I prepared to bid a fond farewell to creatively contained young-sters trapped behind wooden bars (while I dreamed of glorious uninterrupted slumber). It did not go as planned.

Both little dudes hopped into their new digs and snuggled right in. First, they marched over to the futon and re-acclimated all their stuffed toys to their respective beds. Then they snuggled in and demand-ed a bedtime story. (Am I the only mother who has dragged her children from their beds, insisting, "No, YOU WILL come downstairs and play.")

"Noooooo! Brush teeth! Ni ni!" they wailed.

Am I really having this argument?

I bribed them with Cheerios, Goldfish crackers, chicken nuggets, and milk in non-sippy cups. Sure enough, Search took one bite of chicken, spilled his cup all over himself and the seating area, and an-nounced "ALL DONE," as he shoved himself back away from the table. The chair tipped back over and clattered to the ground. Little man's booster chair flew down the sloped mission-style backing, and shot him off the back directly through the center opening of the baby gate and into the living room.

Search lay momentarily still—clearly readying himself for an Academy Award worthy woe-is-me wail. Tears streamed down my face as I snorted and guffawed.

Jon: Are you ok, dude?

Destroy: Milk peeing on chair.

Jon to me: Are you high?

Me: I'm crying over spilt milk.

Search: Bedtime?

We raced through bath time. (More water ended up on the tile floor and on me than in the porcelain tub.) From the bath, we dragged the boys into the living room and forced them to have fun with their new baseball gloves for the remainder of the evening. Finally, Jon uttered the magic words, "You guys ready for bed?"

"YEAH!" chorused the peanut gallery.

Destroy flattened himself back up against the entertainment center. "MOMMEE, WATCH!" He raced forward, vaulting across the little red pedal-car, which went shooting sideways across the room, to complete his gymnastics rotation for the day.

Completely unfazed, he continued his racing toddle toward the stairs and darted upward.

By the time I arrived in the nursery, Destroy was bouncing on his sports-sheeted mattress. Search had removed his pants, found his lovey, and was stubbornly sucking his thumb.

Sleep was debatable. I didn't care. They were in bed, but nary a peep. I was absolutely thrilled.

Then came naps.

The following weekend was our first at having the twins take a nap in their new big-boy beds.

"No nap today, Mommy," declared Destroy, despite the constant eye rubbing and head lolling back against the couch. Search yawned.

I coerced my sons up the stairs with promises of an in-person intimate reading of *Goodnight, Goodnight, Construction Site*. Search snuggled up with My Elle, his *ni-ni lovie*, and contentedly stuck his thumb in his mouth. Destroy decided it would be much more efficient to sit squarely on his pillow and yell (nothing in particular, just loudly).

Once downstairs, I curled up on the couch and began watching the video monitor. (Who needs cable when you've got a live feed into your toddlers' room?) Five minutes into a strength-test of his vocal cords, Search calmly climbed out of his bed and toddled over to his brother. He put his arms around his beloved brother, Destroy, in a hug, which elicited the yells to momentarily transition to screeching squeals.

"Destroy. No yell now. Nap. Ni-ni," Search calmly instructed.

His message adequately shared, Search climbed into his brother's bed, crawled across the length of it, over the railing, and back into his own bed. He resecured My Elle, chugged a bit of water out of his sippy cup, and flopped back down—pulling the pillow over his head.

The yelling ceased. Unfortunately, this did not mean the boys had fallen asleep. I could hear low-decibel mumblings of twin-speak as the two conversed with one another. I occasionally heard a giggle. Neither child was in bed (which meant I could no longer see the shenanigans in progress).

I decided to take a chance and leave them to their own devices. If we weren't going to have naptime, I'd settle for an hour of quiet time spent in their newly furnished big-boy room. (Maybe I'd get lucky and they'd pass out amid the throngs of stuffed animals littered around their floor.)

After a while, the brothers' mutterings got louder. "Puzza!" came a shout, followed by maniacal laughter. (Did I mention the boys' Italian heritage? "Puzza" translates into "stinky.")

"New diaper, I change!" was followed by the distinct sound of a ripping diaper tab.

Naptime was officially over for them and for me. (Code three, people! CODE THREE LIGHTS AND SIRENS!)

I threw the door open and was overcome with the unmistakable pungent aroma of poop. I saw a blur as two toddlers scampered back into bed. Destroy was naked.

Every diaper in the Diaper Genie had been liberated from its wrapper—a trail mix of unwrapped new diapers among their well-worn brethren. Each individual wet-wipe had been removed from the container and strewn about the room—draped across curtains, over stuffed animals, and into pillowcases. I surveyed the carnage.

Search was curled up in the fetal position, innocently blinking back at me, while Destroy stood astride the center of his big-boy bed with a diaper precariously balanced atop his head.

"Mommee, I do it!" he announced proudly.

My fear for the continued existence of naptime for Search and Destroy, and for me, was warranted. (Oh, how the allure of midday sleep is wasted on the young.)

Anyway, we're installing another camera so I can see all angles of the bedroom—notably the diaper pail.

Transcendence

MD Marcus

frustrated by your youth
and curiosity
with quivering energy
that riles me to screams
my words curdle
into unkindness
effervescing cruelties

reflection and conscience
will surely conspire
to multiply my guilt
born out of such
endless failings
a guilt
far outreaching
even your memory

but tonight
I watch you sleep

MD Marcus

my breathing coincides
with the rise and fall of your chest
washing you in silent kisses
that you'll never know were given
and whispering in your ear
that you are the most wonderful
person I know

and I mean it

Tuck In. Turn Off. Pass Out!

Linda Roy

The other night my husband and I both made a mad dash for the closet at the exact same time and simultaneously began ripping our clothes off.

It's not what you think. It was 7 p.m., post dinner and dishes, and while we shared a certain urgency to get horizontal, the only things we let loose were our waistbands. In some sort of systematic, almost choreographed military maneuver, we both dropped trou and reached for our elasticized pajama bottoms.

In an optimistic attempt at clock-out time (that time of day when moms and dads everywhere run to the finish line, or what I like to think of as a shot at sweet relaxation) the reality is a cruel slap in the face of potential slumber.

Although I was one step closer to the news (Have you heard it? I mean *really* heard it? Uninterrupted?), a little bit closer to that favorite TV show, that book on the bedside table, (you know, the one that doesn't rhyme?), we still had to deal with the bedtimes of our beloved offspring.

I love my kids and I enjoy spending time with them. But by the time the sun starts setting, my lids are at half-mast and I'm slack jawed, as in, to gape. I yawn at the mere thought.

The kids urged us to watch "The Krusty Krab Training Video" episode of Sponge Bob for the billionth time, right after we popped them some popcorn and played a few rounds of Skylanders.

For the love of God, I just wanted a cup of tea and a lie down.

Never mind that I spent all day grocery shopping, house cleaning, laundry slinging, and dog wrangling with nary an opportunity for bonbon noshing before the afternoon school bus pulled up. Those bus exhaust fumes always signal the commencement of the party. That's when the after school snack negotiations get underway, ditto the debate over the pros and cons of store bought cookies (I pushed heavily toward that convenient option) vs. homemade personal pan pizzas. (The pizzas win every time.)

And forget the hour I spent with the Food Network between five and six p.m., attempting to craft some sort of culinary masterpiece only to find the cooking show host gazing down at me sympathetically from the television screen as if to say, "Yep. Nailed it!" (in that Internet "nailed it" sort of way). My offering was resolutely rejected by the committee of picky eaters, in favor of boxed mac and cheese, while I silently wished they would just ask me to "Please pack my knives and go" TO BED!

What followed was clean-up time and the doling out of twenty-seven versions of s'mores, (which meant thirty different places I'd find Nutella hidden for days).

Oh, but there wasn't any kicking off of shoes or lounging just yet, because it was time to drag those belligerent children kicking and screaming into the seemingly never ending homework session. They laughed, I cried as I was rocked to my very core by their Common Core math.

And Dad? He'd already given up and adjourned to his man cave.

Time for yet another snack, tooth brushing, PJs, and story time. (Really? The entire Dr. Seuss collection? Can we agree that Mom's tongue is already twisted?)

"Hey! I've got a story for you, kids!"

Mom needs her sleep
She's just exhausted
You jumped on the bed
And she about lost it

Linda Roy

That fourth drink of water
You asked for tonight
Will sit there untouched
You know that she's right
You'll call for her 'cause
You just heard a monster
All she hears are your stallings
You're driving her bonkers
Oh please let your mommy just lie down and rest
It's the right thing to do and mommy knows best
Don't walk in her room during grown up TV
Just lie down and sleep
Please let your mom be
Let her be and you'll see
She'll be much more chipper
She's just on the edge now
Let her get a firm gripper
'Cause sleep's a good thing
Though you may not think so
But as old people get tired-er
Their patience shrinks, yo!
So hop off to bed
Please let your mom doze
Say "good night," drop those lids,
And please keep 'em closed!

Tuck In. Turn Off. Pass Out!

Of course, despite attempted reasoning, hinting, and abject begging, the message inevitably went unheeded.

Last-minute projects needed to be finished. Pictures urgently had to be printed for tomorrow's book report, and requests for the next day's school lunches were then presented (because bringing that up during dinner would have made just too much sense).

And so, when the last cup of water was delivered and that final photo spit out of the printer, when every single minute need was met and we were too spent for anything but unconsciousness . . . finally, blissfully, the promise of sleep was on the horizon.

Wasn't it '60s icon Timothy Leary (or was it Timothy Weary?) who said, "Turn off, tuck in, pass out."

Naptime (or That Which Keeps Me Sane)

Lea Grover

I'm not proud. I'll admit it. I *need* my eighteen-month-old twins to take a nice, long nap each day. I need our regularly scheduled naptime just as much as the children do. I need a few hours in the middle of the afternoon to do my homework: finishing a degree in Administration with two wee ones at home is a challenge. I need time to myself, to drink a hot cup of Jasmine tea, and generally *chillax*. Without a nap, my girls end the day with screaming, flailing, pounding their tiny fists on the floor, and crying over mismatched socks or noodles that aren't perfectly coated in tomato sauce. And while I know better than to throw my spaghetti at the ceiling, I am RIGHT there with them.

That said, naptime hasn't been going well.

I'd like to blame Grandma. She was here for a week and was happy to go into the nursery to comfort one of my twins, Deborah, who panicked because the door was closed; and to cuddle Sophia, her twin sister, when she started gnawing on the bars of her crib like a lunatic. Grandma was all too willing to bend to the will of my terroristic toddlers, to set a precedent of chaos. But it's not fair to blame Grandma.

I'd like to blame Sophie. The damned roseola virus that she got woke her up in the night and left her tired at odd hours of the day, effectively screwing up her routine. I'd like to say Deborah's just going along for the nap-free ride, but that's not fair either.

The reason my twins aren't napping is because they are having *too much fun.* My daughters are best friends. And like most little girls in a room with their best friend, they would rather play than sleep.

Naptime used to be elegant in its simplicity. I would change diapers, read a story, tuck the girls into their quilts, make sure they had their frog lovies, and turn on a lullaby CD. Then I'd leave the room to enjoy my statistics-class homework and a decaf Earl Grey, in peace.

My children would nap for 150 minutes: *two-and-a-half* glorious hours, my favorite time of day. It was magical, a fairy tale come true.

Naptime (or That Which Keeps Me Sane)

Now I change diapers, read a story, and tuck the girls in with their quilts and frogs. I turn on the lullabies and leave the room. And the next hour is filled with the sound of raucous laughter.

I go in every twenty minutes or so with an angry shush, re-tuck (HILARIOUS according to Deborah), and tell everyone to be quiet and go to sleep.

This does not work.

The only thing I can do is rock them to sleep. It's something that, while very sweet, we haven't done in nine months. They're a hell of a lot bigger now. I cannot rock both toddlers at once; it's physically impossible. First of all, they're made out of knees. Second of all, the moment they see each other on my lap they realize they are so much closer together than in their cribs, and they can have more fun this way. Even getting poked in the eye is funny if you're sharing your mother's lap.

Therefore, I rock them one at a time. I throw a quilt over Deborah's head, as though she were a parrot, and rock her while Sophie, a mere 18 inches away, screams, laughs, and calls "Debba! Debba! Debba!" over and over again. When I put Deborah in her crib, somehow snoring peacefully despite the sister-induced chaos, I attempt to soothe Sophie, who's wired from the effort of trying to figure out what the hell happened to her best friend.

They can't control their constant yawning as they play in their cribs, and every fifteen minutes or so they lie down and *nearly* fall asleep. Sometimes Sophie actually passes out during these breaks, but Deborah wakes her up by chucking a toy at her head (once she even pulled the sheet off her crib for this purpose), and after a few seconds of angry whining the game is BACK ON!

I have not been taking this turn of events gracefully. I have shouted, thrown my children into their cribs (they find this very funny), taken away toys, and cranked up the volume on the white noise. I have begged, and I've been extremely rude to my husband when he's home through this charade. In short, I've acted like somebody who really needs a nap.

This is not productive.

I don't know why my children's mirthful determination not to sleep incites such a rage in me, but it does. Half an hour into this ridiculous routine, I am beside myself with frustration and exhaustion. I'm ready to slam doors and throw cold and un-drunk cups of tea through panes of glass.

It used to be like clockwork—regardless of what time they started their day, when 12:30 p.m. came, my daughters passed out where they stood. If we were in a restaurant, or watching cartoons, or in the car, I'd see them yawn with their eyes drooping and say to myself, "Gosh! It must be 12:30!" And lo and behold—it was. If we were driving, I struggled to keep Sophie awake until we got home, lest I accidently wake her putting her to bed before the magic of the nap had done its work.

Now? If I'm lucky, they pass out right around the time their naps used to end. But instead of waking up lazily and happily, they get up totally pissed about having slept through a meal. It's painful. But, I tell myself, at least *they're* enjoying themselves.

Still, no matter how much I want to throttle one of them, when I'm rocking my girls and they're laughing uproariously, poking my nose, pulling my hair, stealing my glasses, or sticking their fingers in my ear—once they're asleep and I'm holding their tiny, unconscious bodies in my arms, looking at their gorgeous eyelashes and marveling at the unfathomable softness of their squishy cheeks; once it's peaceful and quiet and the laughter has stopped and a truncated nap begins, it feels like the first time I ever held them. I fall in love with those beautiful faces and sweet, sleepy breathing sounds all over again.

And then I feel like a giant jerk (a giant jerk that needs a cup of tea and a timeout, and maybe a nap).

Excerpts from
Life on the Ranch
Diane Tolley

Bunk Bed Bliss

Before Grant and I married and my two children were born, I had a fantastic sleep, the best sleep of my life. It happened when I was eight. Dad had taken my brothers out on an overnight. My older sister, Chris, and I saw an opportunity for some fun and adventure. My brothers' wonderful bunk bed, in the bedroom next to mine, stood empty. *We would stay the night in our brothers' beds!* (I should mention I had long coveted their beds. They were made of beautiful, solid maple and were *soooo* comfortable.)

Chris took the upper bunk and I snuggled into the lower one and we talked and laughed until mom made a couple of visits to the doorway: first she threatened to separate us if we didn't quiet down, and then she threatened to send us back to our own beds (shudder). It was this second warning that made me finally give up and close my eyes. Later my shoulder started to ache.

When I opened my eyes sunlight streamed into the room. At first, I didn't recognize it for what it was. I had never seen the world go from black to light quite so dramatically. I thought someone had switched on the lamp. I turned to look at the window.

Nope. I was right. It was sunlight. Somehow, morning had instantly followed bedtime.

It took some time for me to realize that I had just had a night of deep, dreamless sleep. I know it happens to other people, but it had never happened before (or since).

But I have that one night. And, believe me, in the sleepless-mom hours between midnight and 4:00 a.m., I often think of it.

Where's a bunk bed when you need it?

Sleep Construction

Shortly after Grant and I were married, he took a job as foreman at a housing plant where they built prefabricated homes. He was good at his job, and it was two minutes from where we lived.

Living so close, he came home for lunch every day.

Excerpts from *Life on the Ranch*

For me, his new bride, life was perfect. But for Grant it wasn't. His job was very stressful. He had too many bosses, several without any knowledge of building. But he carried on for two years. After all, he had a family to feed.

But the stress started to show. He developed health issues. He stopped sleeping.

He started making noises about going back to school. Grant had been in school when we started dating, but had quit to take a job after we were married. He'd realized that he had made a mistake and wanted to correct it.

I was unconvinced. How would we provide for ourselves if we had no income?

He continued on, growing more and more unhappy and sleeping less and less.

Once, in the middle of the night, he snorted, sat up on the edge of the bed, and started getting dressed.

"Honey, where are you going?" I asked. "It's 4:00 a.m."

He jumped up and looked around. "Oh," he said. "Oh."

He pulled off his shirt, lay back down, and was instantly snoring.

Is there a term for sleep-dressing?

Another night, around 3:00 a.m., I slept quietly. Suddenly, Grant shot up in bed, grabbed me by the collar of my pajamas, pulled me to a sitting position and shouted, "You hold the ladder! I'll nail the soffit!" My sleep-fogged brain vaguely registered that these were "house-building" terms.

"Honey, you're dreaming," I said, rather shakily. "Go back to sleep."

But he wasn't to be deterred and shook me slightly. "Okay?"

"Okay!" I said.

"Good." He dropped me and flopped back onto the bed. Seconds later, I could hear his soft snore. He had been asleep the whole time. I, however, would probably never sleep again.

I was finally convinced. Grant went back to school and studied history, arts, and anthropology. He eventually earned a doctorate degree.

His health improved, as did his sleeping habits: he no longer sleep-dressed (or roughed up his wife). And you can bet that the installation of any soffit was in broad daylight, with real hammers (and real soffit, for that matter).

Going back to school turned out to be a good decision (though with a new family to provide for, it had seemed anything but at the time). And sometimes I wonder if he was really asleep. It just took some convincing of said wife.

Sleep and the Slow Journey to Justice

Beth Markley

At a wee hour in the night, not so long ago, when sixteen-month-old Colin stood at my bedside, he only had to softly clear his throat before I opened my eyes. *Oh, hello little person.* Then I was wide awake. The fact that this kid was here meant he had climbed from his crib and over the baby gate that was secured AT THE TOP OF THE STAIRS. I pulled him into bed, dooming us all to a night of severely interrupted sleep unless somebody moved to the couch by morning. Our queen bed was big enough for two adults, but not the addition of one toddler sleep gymnast.

Each of our boys started out life sleeping in our bedroom, eventually moving to their own room at three or four months old.

One night before our youngest had migrated to his own quarters, I heard his dad shuffling into the bathroom. There was a second of silence, then a crash. The baby screamed and started howling in his bassinet. I made it to the bathroom door in one leap.

"What the . . . YOU WOKE UP THE BABY!" I yelled at my poor husband, who was lying on the floor having fainted after locking his knees like a groomsman at the altar. Never mind that he could have conked his head on the tub and died right there, *he had robbed me of sleep.*

Eventually, each kid moved to his own room, and then from a crib to a regular bed. But still, for years, when the kids were little, we found ourselves with one or both of them in bed with us.

Sleeping with a baby or toddler is one of the sweetest things I know of: drifting off with a warm little body cuddled up next to me, his hair smelling like chamomile baby shampoo, followed by waking in the slow realization that I'm snoozing in a warm puddle because someone's diaper leaked, or to a little foot jamming my nose into my skull.

My kids were hard on my husband and me (as are most kids on their parents). At some point during the day, they could act on the impulse to start a fire in our living room, cut holes in my couch cushions with scissors, or sneak a container full of slugs into the house. Then there's this whole need for vigilance at night lest someone tumble down the stairs on his way to snuggle with us.

Still, I knew the time would come when no one would be sneaking in bed for a midnight cuddle. I looked forward to a full night's sleep, maybe a few in a row, actually, but I also knew I would miss the little warm body curled up next to me.

Today, I have no more toddlers to pull me out of sleep. If I'm awake at odd hours, it's because of a stray thought: *When was the last time my husband changed the batteries in the fire alarm?*

One recent morning I had given up trying to fall back to sleep and came across an Internet article about a Duke University study showing how women need more sleep than men, and how we suffer more mentally and physically from sleep deprivation. *Huh?*

The article didn't say how much more sleep we needed, but I'm sure it's more than I've been able to get on a consistent basis at any time over the past fifteen years.

Come to think of it, this lack of sleep thing is probably why the adult women I grew up with seemed so much grouchier when I was a kid than they do today. (This probably has a lot to do with why I'm a complete crank most of the time now.)

It was only a short time ago that our two boys and their habit of disrupting our nights were the reason I would have a regular meltdown every day about mid-afternoon when the coffee wore off.

The days of nighttime visits are behind us (teenagers and preteens need way more sleep, and never, ever seem to want to cuddle). But our nighttime interruptions continue. Not only am I likely to be jolted awake by an early morning brain spin, I am also likely to be kept up too late waiting for some young person to get home from a night out with friends.

But there are moments of sweet justice.

This weekend we sprang a surprise movie night on the kids. It had been a weekend jam-packed with disappointment: our fridge broke and needed to be replaced, and the resulting fridge shopping preempted a family trip to the ski hill (which is how we found ourselves at a conciliatory late screening of *The Hobbit* on a Sunday night, then home, crawling into bed around midnight, followed by a lot of grouching on Monday morning before school).

"Not enough sleep," my bleary-eyed fourteen-year-old said to me, apparently robbed of his ability to form complete sentences by virtue of fewer than six hours of shut-eye. "Can I stay home from school today?"

"Nope. You must sally forth with enthusiasm and pep, to face your day."

I reveled for a bit in that moment. Then I took a nap.

Ten Steps to Become "Sleeperstitious"

Lisa Carmody Doiron

I'm done thinking my kid is going to grasp the art of a good night's sleep. I'm through with the science of sleep training. I have become "sleeperstitious" to the point of being a total whack-job cliché. When all else fails, and superstition is all a mom has left to rely on, I say, "Do it." (Stevie Wonder was wrong when he said, "Superstition ain't the way.") So I've devised ten easy steps to help tired moms become "sleeperstitious."

Step #1: After a sleepless night, get in your car and go to the drive thru and order a giant, sloppy coffee.

"That'll be $3.71!" the overly perky server will say.

Drive to the window and purposely give her the EXACT change. Why? Because you KNOW she's going to give you back the penny and tell you she doesn't need it, even though she told you your giant cup of Heaven costs exactly $3.71.

Step #2: When she gives you back the penny you just handed her, gasp, "A lucky penny!" Then exclaim, "I need to make a wish! I wish for my adorable, highly intelligent baby to start sleeping through the goddamn night!"

Step #3: Throw the penny into your cup holder full of change as though it were a wishing well.

Step #4: Squeal out of the drive thru for dramatic psycho-mother effect, in the hopes that the same kid is working tomorrow morning so you can perform the whole charade again.

Step #5: Later that night, when your baby wakes up at 11 p.m. for the first of four night feedings, wait until precisely 11:11 p.m. Then walk into the kitchen, grasp both sides of the oven, and speak directly to the clock. "Clock, for the love of all things good and holy, make this baby sleep. I'll give up half of his intelligence and a quarter of his good looks just for a morsel of sleep. Do it, 11:11. DO IT. Make it happen."

Step #6: Want to know how 11:11 will respond? It will respond by turning 11:12 before you can even finish your plea EVERY TIME!

Stupid, goddamned oven clock.

Ten Steps to Become "Sleeperstitious"

Step #7: Pretend you're Audrey Hepburn in *Breakfast at Tiffany's*. (That's a real superstition, isn't it?) Wrap a towel around your head and sit on your windowsill and sing "Moon River" over and over and over again. Get out your ukulele and play it poorly, on purpose, just to be authentic to the movie.

Step #8: Look up and secretly hope a hunk is staring back at you; however, instead, you'll see stars, stars, and more stars because it's the goddamn middle of the goddamn night, and the baby won't goddamn sleep. So you pick a star, a lucky one, the luckiest one of all, and make your wish.

Step #9: When you peek down at your ukulele strings (because you're too rusty to change chords without looking), you will lose your lucky star in the sky. *Which one was it?! They're all so bright and shiny. Which one is the lucky one?!*

Now your wish will never come true.

Step #10: Give up on the stars and decide to drink a lucky glass of wine instead, maybe two. And by two, I mean a box. Drink a box of wine because when art, science, and "sleeperstition" fail you, you've still got wine.

What Mommies Need (Hint: It's Not Sex)

Shannon Lell

I spent my days at home with a toddler and a breast-feeding infant who'd wake up every night around midnight and cry for two or three hours while his father slept in the guest bedroom. After a 2:00 a.m. nursing I'd go back to bed and put my head on my pillow, only to hear my toddler start crying, and it would reduce me to tears in a matter of seconds.

Each night I'd pray with hopeful optimism that *tonight* would be the night my baby would not wake up at midnight and cry for three hours or that my two-year-old would not wake up after him and start crying too.

By the end of the third month, I was out-of-my-mind insane with the need for sleep. It had defined my every waking moment, my every thought and emotion: how much I needed it, when was I was going to get it, how long would I have it, and please let it be more than forty-five minutes.

I couldn't make sense of daily life anymore, especially my desire to write it all out and understand its meaning (as if putting pen to paper would make it all clear again).

One particular night, as I sat there in a heap of bone tiredness writing and listening to my son wail in the dark, Maslow and his Hierarchy of Needs Theory crept into my consciousness.

I first heard of Maslow in my high school health class during my sophomore year. My teacher, who was also the wrestling coach, was a stout, burly man with a stomach as hard as a kettle drum. He used to `walk up and down the aisle with a crooked, bow-legged wrestler's limp and peer over our shoulders during tests. His style of instruction was intimidating and declarative: "You can still get pregnant even if the girl is currently menstruating, don't you know, kids?" Then he'd sneer at us with a knowing look while we fidgeted in our small plastic chairs (he was informative *and* slightly traumatizing).

The next time I came across Maslow's Hierarchy of Needs Theory was in a college psychology course. It's a theory that pertains to human growth and development. Maslow came up with this theory by studying what he called "exemplary people" like

What Mommies Need (Hint: It's Not Sex)

Albert Einstein and Eleanor Roosevelt. His goal was to uncover the principles behind basic human motivations and to better understand why people will seek out certain experiences in their respective environments.

In his hierarchy, the bottom of the pyramid represents our everyday basic needs: air, food, water, sleep, and pooping. It also lists "sex" in that category. As you ascend the pyramid, you come to things like love, belonging, esteem and self-actualization—a fulfilled understanding of the meaning of your life.

This theory stuck with me, but I had no need for it until I became an insane, sleep-deprived mom. But it wasn't the prioritizing of *other people's needs* that inspired me to contemplate Maslow's theory (the little people in my house were doing just fine getting *their needs* met). *I was the one* lacking sleep, adequate sustenance, and water—partly due to the demands of breastfeeding.

Having a baby stripped my life down to its most basic elements. All those layers of hard-won self-esteem, accomplishments, and the loving relationship I built with my spouse, they all exited the building along with my placenta.

Days after birthing a precious baby, I slid back to the lowest rungs of the human growth ladder.

I became a shadow of my former self, begging and pleading for basic necessities like sleep, food, water, and elimination (because pooping after a vaginal birth is something no one ever told me about, but should NOT go without its fair share of warnings! *Why didn't you teach me that in high school, Mr. Health Teacher?*).

In the seconds it took the doctor to place my baby on my chest, like a lightning bolt I understood with a fierce profundity the meaning of my life. If there was ever a moment at the pinnacle of human growth, it was the moment I looked into my child's eyes for the very first time. In the days that followed, I began to free-fall, like rain through a gutter, back down the ladder of human growth until I was a milky puddle on the floor, begging for someone to bring me a sandwich and give me five minutes of sleep.

And I can say for certain, Mr. Maslow, that sex is NOT a basic need. For goodness sakes man, what were you thinking? Really? Sex is equal to breathing?

As a part-time, work-at-home mother, everyone around me needed something from me every second of my day. I found myself constantly evaluating which needs were priorities and which could wait. On sleepless nights I began writing about it in an attempt to understand why I felt so crazy all the time, as if putting pen to paper would make it all clear again. I questioned my priorities: *Should I rock his crib—it never gets him back to sleep. It just speeds up the waking process. Should I continue to write? Should I attempt to get some sleep? Or is my need to write more important than my baby's need to sleep (or my need for sleep)?*

Six months postpartum I recognized myself again. I peered in the mirror and glimpsed the crooked shape of my eyebrows, the natural color of my hair, and two legs that looked like the pelt of a stuffed dead animal. I also saw a woman who thought about more than just the color and consistency of her baby's poop, and I wanted to be that woman again: to use my brain for more than just calculating the time it took me to make a grocery run as opposed to the next scheduled nap.

Maslow says self-actualizing is the highest rung of the human needs and motivational pyramid: the part that yearns to be creative, to think, and to give meaning to life.

I lacked one of my most basic needs: sleep, and yet, in the face of pure exhaustion, I was still writing, attempting to be creative, and searching for meaning in my life.

Many months (and many hours of consolidated sleep) later, I can see the flaw in Maslow's Theory (and not just the sex part). Maslow might have studied Einstein, but he didn't study mommies. As a mom I am capable of *building* pyramids in the time it takes to nurse a newborn. I'm not superhuman, but in the face of my child, I am capable of doing superhuman things.

In the midst of the physical and emotional energy required to have babies and raise them, meaning can be the hardest to hold on to. It lives on the top of the pyramid while mommies like me are down on the floor eating spilled mac-n-cheese because it was in arm's reach and it didn't require getting up.

I felt crazy all the time because *I longed for meaning* but couldn't find it due to lack of significant shut-eye.

So I propose a new Hierarchy of Needs Theory, shaped like a heart for us moms. At the center would be sleep. A little farther out would be food, water, and all those people who love us most: our support system. After that we'll include hygiene and self-esteem. The outer layer of the heart (the part that makes everything inside worth it) would be children's giggles, bedtime snuggles, fat baby thighs, and toothless grins.

What Mommies Need (Hint: It's Not Sex)

Maybe on the outside of the heart, in its own little triangle, sex can be included (because a girl can still get pregnant even if she is menstruating, or breast-feeding, didn't you know that?).

See? informative *and* traumatizing.

Waiting Around (after "Walking Around" by Pablo Neruda)

Trish Hopkinson

It so happens, I am tired of being a woman.
And it happens while I wait for my children to grow
into the burning licks of adulthood. The streaks
of summer sun have gone,

drained between gaps into gutters,
and the ink smell of report cards and recipe boxes
cringes me into corners. Still, I would be satisfied
if I could draw from language,
the banquet of poets.

If I could salvage the space in time
for thought and collect it
like a souvenir. I can no longer
be timid and quiet, breathless

and withdrawn.
I can't salve the silence.
I can't be this vineyard
to be bottled, corked,
cellared, and shelved.

That's why the year-end gapes with pointed teeth,
growling at my crow's feet,
and gravelling into my throat.
It claws its way through the edges of an age
I never planned to reach

and diffuses my life into dullness—
workout rooms and nail salons,
bleach-white sheets on clotheslines,
and treacherous photographs of younger me
at barbecues and birthday parties.

I wait. I hold still in my form-fitting camouflage.
I put on my strong suit and war paint lipstick
and I gamble on what's expected.
And what to become. And how
to behave: mother, wife, brave.

Originally published by Wicked Banshee Press in *Issue #2 Fall 2014*. October 2014.

Whatever, Sleep Deprivation

Jean Heffernan

Complaining about sleep deprivation is ridiculous. Yeah, I said it. I'm throwing down the gauntlet (or pillow) because I need to suck it up and learn to embrace sleep deprivation as a busy-all-the-time adult. It's doing me a lot of favors and I am neglecting to recognize that. (Sleep deprivation is doing me a favor, not throwing pillows. Throwing pillows is fun, but does not benefit me in any way.)

I would be a superstar constantly because not sleeping is rocking my world (all those doctors and researchers and lab studies about fatigue don't know squat).

Doctors tell me sleep regression is supposed to make me dumber. Fine with me! I don't want to understand why our government is so screwed up. It's only going to make me more depressed. Ignorance is bills. *Bliss*, I meant *bliss*.

I've read articles appealing to my vanity by mentioning that sleep deprivation is supposed to prematurely age my skin. Not sleeping *has* turned my crow's feet into Grand Canyons on either side of my face. That's fine. I won't be able to walk the runways at Mercedes Benz Fashion Week, and that's a good thing because participating through Project Runway Marathons on my couch is way more fun.

I'm not swayed to slumber when I hear that lack of sleep is supposed to kill sex drive. Yes, the sex drive is six feet under and that's saving me tons of money on birth control and razors to shave my legs. Interesting side effect of that: we have lower heating costs because I'm wearing permanent leg warmers. Don't sleep and turn down the heat! Go green!

We need a motto for this sleepless mommy movement. And HELLO, I already have one because I have so much more time on my hands now that I don't sleep!

I stenciled it on the wall of my bedroom, except I don't call it a bedroom; I call it a waiting room (as in I'm waiting to party with my kids all night instead of sleeping in my bed). So what if I'm making my prefrontal cortex work harder by not sleeping? It gives my temporal lobe a break.

What about sleep deprivation impairing immune function? Perhaps it was sleep deprivation that gave me three years of constant colds. I have supported the families of countless starving doctors across two states (philanthropy much?) and as a result, I am immune to everything now. I can't even get Botox because I'm immune to botulism.

Lab studies done on rats have shown that severe sleep deprivation can cause death or inability to heal wounds. Listen, I know we share 99 percent of our DNA with rats, but we have a very special 1 percent all to ourselves and that's called coffee. (Don't worry about us moms, scientists. Coffee always makes our mornings, afternoons, and *who cares if it's 6:00 p.m.* evenings better.)

So what if lack of sleep suppresses growth hormones? I have an established wardrobe dating back to 1998. I have vintage grunge I need to wear. If I grow, I won't be able to wear my distressed jeans and Doc Martens. Lack of sleep is helping me preserve my wardrobe.

Sleepiness can harm my memory and disrupt my ability to hold on to routines, *which is awesome because I like to shake it up a bit.* Story time starts at 9:30 or maybe 10:00. We alternate between the two on a weekly basis. (You never know when crazy mama's showing up to story time at the library!) Toddlers and preschoolers don't need routine and consistency. They thrive on unpredictability and chaos.

Don't worry that lack of sleep can cause mistakes or flakiness. At dinner, I can't find the milk I put on the table even if it's right in front of my face. Well, I needed some exercise. Walking needlessly into the kitchen only to return to the dinner table because that's where the milk was all along is beneficial.

I was really concerned about irritability when I became immersed in the sleeplessness culture. I fretted that no one would love me when I was cranky all the time. To my delight, I discovered that irritability is probably the best part about it! Sleeplessness means irritability, and that means I don't give a crap.

Other things I don't give a crap about anymore: 1) My appearance. My hair looks like I washed it in the garbage disposal but I don't care because we got to school on time. 2) Being angry in public: I told the lady with the huge dinosaur car that it's not actually okay to take up part of my parking spot in the crowded school parking lot. "Baby girl's got to get in her car seat and we're not waiting for you to finish a fifteen-minute conversation with the teacher." *It doesn't matter if this lady loves me.* 3) The Pinterest-beauty of my house: I have energy for one thing and I can choose to play in the leaves with my kids or rake them. *Play. Play every time.* It's a bonus benefit for the kids and me. 4) Not giving a crap is the key to raising healthy children.

I embrace my lack of sleep. It's doing me a favor, a HUGE favor. One day my kids will thank me for it. They will thank me for it via a stolen-moment phone call while balancing their baby on a whirring washing machine because "I-swear-mom-it's-the-only-thing-that-calms-her-down." And my wrinkly eyes will crinkle more and the corners of my mouth will turn up to reveal a coffee-yellow-toothed smile on my face in appreciation of their news. I know it will make me happy.

My parents are proof. They smile at my stories all the time.

Sleep Deprivation Sucks

Michelle Grewe

Falling asleep became an impossible task after I had kids. The Sandman skipped my house as if dead-cattle butter was smeared over the doorway.

I fed a newborn every two hours while trying to maintain a house and cook meals—followed by two more newborns.

It took me ten times longer to brush my teeth or wash the dishes. Brilliant ideas became irrational and stupid—making me look like the village drunk.

I fell asleep at work while doing brainless tasks like putting postage stamps on receivables: only to wake up and find half the stamps were placed dead center on the envelope.

I took notes in class only to wake up and see "The psychosexual stages are comprised of—bat wings and Mark's accounting entries for the soufflé . . ." scribbled in my notebook.

One time my car was stopped in the McDonald's drive thru, between window number one and window number two. Traffic slowly moved up and I inched toward window number two until my six-year-old daughter screamed, "Mommy look out!" I damn near drove into a brick building three inches in front of me.

My oldest child (who was born on the autism spectrum) operated on a thirty-hour day. Some days she slept for most of the night, and other days she didn't sleep at all.

Later we learned my youngest daughter was allergic to milk and soy. For the first two years of her life her arms and legs were covered in a blood-drawing itchy rash. If the itching wasn't enough to keep her awake at night, the antihistamines the doctors pushed made her more hyperactive.

At night I slept fifteen minutes here, forty-five minutes there. I napped only at my husband's mercy. And he didn't have much. When I wasn't sleeping I was chasing my kids and bouncing off the trampoline to get a *blankie*. I practiced Jet Li stunts to get one kid out of the space between the sofa and the wall. (I didn't think it was humanly possible to fit behind there, but I can tell you it is.) Sometimes I'd lie on the floor with soap-dripping scrubbers in my hands, huddled over a trashcan, throwing up while my kids screamed and pulled hair over a toy.

I felt insulted when someone said, "I didn't sleep last night either. I got up three times in the middle of the night." (If you got up, you went to sleep. You don't get to claim not sleeping. I didn't sleep because I never lay down.)

I suffered daily migraines: show-stopping, vomit-inducing—*someone shoot me in the head and end the pain*—migraines. I lost over eighty pounds.

I was irritable. I wept over hair loss and scraps of toilet paper dropped on the bathroom floor. I had raging hormonal teenagers inside my skin.

Sleep deprivation was like having lice that carried the swine flu. It was enough to put me on suicide watch at the local loony farm.

The worst part of my sleep deprivation? Nobody cared. My husband was like a fourth kid. My mother took care of my older sister's children. My younger sister was too busy not having her own. I felt alone and abandoned.

Then I found mom blogs. They became my daily inspiration. The friends I made online were a godsend. They let me gripe about the daily grind, offered encouraging words, and cyber hugs. Someone, somewhere over the rainbow and beneath the pale moonlight cared.

Today, keeping up with the kids and maintaining my house and my health feels overwhelming with no solution in sight, but I sleep regularly now and am well rested enough to face the day with a clear mind (with the help of my inner bi*** and sleeping pills).

To all the sleep-deprived moms of the world: I want to say, "Stop reading this and go to bed, and if you can't fall asleep, I know some mom bloggers on the Internet I can introduce you to."

Case

Tamara Woods

PenPaperPad.com

Stuffed with two pillows, pink afghan
spilling out of its side.
Shag green carpet
dug into my earnest knees.
Tears clogged my voice,
I read from my steno pad.
Written first in diary,
then in the pad,
edited, rewritten,
Edited again.
Until Mom's weary eyes closed,
And my voice trembled
Because I had to get the words out
Right then.
Immediacy of youth.
Are you listening?
Repeat what I said.
She'd sleepily respond,
Remembering words a line
from before she drifted off

Tamara Woods

To tomorrow's day:
bedpans and call lights.
Lifting and bending.
Aching and choking on frustration.
Now those eyes,
lined in black
Sagging from weariness
Weight of six-person family
pressing her into
sagging mattress.
Beyond exhausted,
still, she listened.

The Gift of Temporary Exhaustion

Jessica Cantrell

I was eighteen when my first daughter was born. I languished in bed, stroking her sweet, silky baby skin, and watched wide-eyed as her mouth worked my nipple like a pump. I felt like a queen. I might have bathed in milk. I slept often, when she slept, not because it was smart but because I felt like it. When we woke up, we smiled together, fresh.

Sometime in her second year, there was a growing chill to the air, a bare, frank nervousness I felt compelled to tuck away, out of caution. I chose not to talk about it, afraid I'd be found out for the obvious louse of a mother I must have become. Instead, I strove to fix it. *Balance must be reclaimed.* I wanted to be infallible. I wanted to be royalty again.

In the middle of her third year, I was wretched with unease. The tedious, endless cycle of being home with her wore out a vibrant layer of my being.

It didn't help that I was still not twenty, still not whole in my own becoming. I felt stunted, off balance, teetering on some unknown brink. I stayed up late to read, and write, and watch dark dramas on television. I worried it all into shadows, where it cowered with me, unnerved, until my daughter turned three and a half and decided she was too old to nap.

I held that time precious. It was one of too few hours I was allowed to exist without a necessary and undeniable attachment to another being; the pulsing throb of my own responsibility faded into something resembling a heartbeat, and I was free to plug away at mundane life or to sit, trembling slightly with emotion, until I found my glow again. I needed that nap more than she did, I'm sure. And so I fought it.

Normally she'd lie on my stomach, and I'd rub her back and sing a medley of old songs I hoped she'd remember fondly someday. But this time I lay in that humid room, silent except for the whir of the fan and my singing voice—shaky with panic. The energy was so thick I could *feel* it: hers was so obviously un-sleepy and mine was desperate. I was maddened by it.

I quivered with petty jealousy for childless friends who were rife with freedom, and untethered save for the animals they treated as children. They arrived home at seven o'clock from their work commutes and threw themselves onto beds and couches, complaining of tiredness. I felt so old, so uncool, and yet I meant every bleak, haughty word: *"You don't know tired."*

This level of exhaustion could only be compelled by death, disease, or depression—some inner darkness that worked out in the impossible, deceitful hours of night. I know this from my own experiences of dark.

But I won't compare being mother-tired to all of that. For me it was a choosy sort of sickness that would eventually be cured by the simple and drastic passing of time.

My youngest daughter was born a year later, and she woke me a couple of times a night to remind herself she's not alone. Her bedroom was above mine, and my partner and I slept without the white-noise-comfort of our fan so we'd hear her orphan call in the dark.

It was always the first, pitiful little yelp that brought me to attention, and the second that sprung me to my feet, awake and keen with purpose.

Passing through the kitchen on my way to the stairs, I snuck a glance at the clock, if I was brave:

11:30, midnight, 3 a.m. I vaulted up the first steps, the old wood creaking, and then I slowed. Her voice was teetering: the noise of a small, needy thing in the night who knew its mother would come. My toes felt for the last step. I paused. She was drowning in want, and I was the one who opened the door, smiling with my answer: "Hush, now. I am here."

In the mornings there are bags under my eyes. They're relatively new, having arrived the year after she was born, and they have yet to depart. They're very wholly mine, and like the other marks on my body, I've grown comfortable with them. They're new friends that feel old, as old as I sometimes feel, though I'm only twenty-four now. They are the physical, unavoidable reminders that my children have changed me, and the warnings for times to come.

There will be a time when I will languish in bed at some hour as insane and unthinkable as ten in the morning. Years of apologetic self-care will have eased the under-eye circles, though there will be new wrinkles to fret over, if I please. There will be no POUNDING of small, hobbit-like feet on the floorboards, *one-two-three,* above, no commanding call to battle, "HEY! HEY! MUMMA!"

I will close my eyes and clench my heart against the missing-of-them, for those noises will be gone and my babies with them. Sleep will be my friend again, if I'll have it. Until then, I'm happy to be fully exhausted. I have the balm of baby skin, the peals of girl-child laughter, potty training and its humor and various unsophisticated smells. I have warm, needy bodies to cuddle—as closely as possible—and tiny sidekicks. I have instant grins to match my own, bubble baths with too much bubble mixture, and small, eager hands putting too many mini-marshmallows in their hot chocolate. I have extra bedtime kisses, deserving of many trips back downstairs. I have clinging hugs that don't want to let go. I have churning, ravenous minds and untarnished hearts. I have everything.

And it's worth it.

About the Contributors

Allison Carter, Go Dansker Mom: Allison is a content strategist and freelance writer. She has happily made a career out of writing content, blogging, speaking at conferences, and consulting. But her heart is in her creative career. She blogs regularly(ish) at Go Dansker Mom. It is a wild ride with heartfelt pieces on parenting, Martha Moments, lists, tips, recipes, cocktails, and whatever else modern moms think about. She has two boys and is happily married. Her sometimes dirt-and-bug-filled writing has appeared on Scary Mommy, What The Flicka?, Mampedia, Mamalode, Mom365, and in the anthology *The HerStories Project: Women Explore the Joy, Pain and Power of Female Friendship*, and even in the local newspapers. (godanskermom.com)

Amy Denby, Dear Babies: Amy is a former entertainment editor of *Seventeen* and *More* magazines where she wrote book and movie reviews. She also was a copywriter and photo producer for J.Crew. Today she is home with her preschool-age twins, trying not to step on Legos barefoot, because that really hurts. Her book of letters, *Dear Babies*, is based on her blog of the same name and is available on Amazon. (amydenby.com)

Andrea Bates, Good Girl Gone Redneck: Andrea is a native New Yorker living in NC who has become quite accustomed to wearing flip flops year-round. An LCSW, she spends her free time volunteering and advocating for mental health awareness. At her blog, Good Girl Gone Redneck, Andrea writes from the heart, sharing the ins and outs of parenting, family, and life. Andrea has been featured on Scary Mommy, SITS, Postpartum Progress, and Carolina Parent. She lives in Durham with her husband, daughter, two dogs, two cats, and trillions of dust bunnies. She hopes to find a clear surface in her house in the coming decade. (goodgirlgoneredneck.com)

Anna Gragert, Just Stay Gold Okay: When Anna Gragert isn't trying to create a groundbreaking third-person bio for herself, she's writing, reading fiction for Cactus Heart Press, or catering to her little black cat.

Follow @Anna_Gragert on Twitter to keep up with her adventures in all things human/creative. (juststaygoldokay.wordpress.com)

Annie Swingen, Swirleytime: Annie is a communications professional, freelance writer, and blogger living the dream in Chicago, IL. She keeps herself occupied penning humorous posts about her strong-willed preschooler, nerdy husband, and high-maintenance (and often unreasonable) mother. She also enjoys writing about anything that strikes her as odd or total BS. Find Annie on Facebook and Twitter, in the parenting section of the Chicago Tribune, published in humorous parenting anthologies, and on her ChicagoNow blogs, Swirleytime, and Cradle to Grave Caregiving. (chicagonow.com/swirleytime)

Beth Markley, Manic Mumbling, Musings of a Mostly Mediocre Mom: Beth is a forty-something freelance consultant and overcommitted volunteer. She has a wonderful family, which puts up with her use of their exploits as blog fodder. That family (and fodder) includes a husband with a fantastic sense of humor and two sons (teen and preteen) who will one day appreciate it. Beth loves writing, reading, and running long distances very slowly. She consistently overestimates her abilities as a chef. She shouldn't be allowed to dye her own hair or pick out living room furniture, and she can't figure out the TV remote, but is otherwise a good person. If she could choose any superpower, it would be the ability to read in a moving vehicle without getting woozy. Her work has been featured online at Scary Mommy, What The Flicka?, and Erma Bombeck Writers' Workshop. (manicmumbling.com)

Cordelia Newlin de Rojas, Multilingual Mama: Cordelia is the voice behind the site Multilingual Mama where she chronicles her parenting adventures in raising her two global girls abroad. Former hobnobber with the intellectual elite, she formerly resided in Bangkok, Thailand where she home schooled her children, protected her registered dog from stray pythons, and Indiana Jonesed her way through the urban jungle. Cordelia's eclectic and often regrettable past includes eco-innovation, sailing instruction, and papermaking. She is a regular contributor to In Culture Parent, BLUNTmoms, and has been published on Fast Company. When she isn't writing, Cordelia is creating multilingual citizens of the world, one child at a time. (multilingualmama.com)

Desiree Roundtree, The Bklyn Times: Desiree is a freelance writer, blogger, and professional know-it-all. She is the author of several short stories including "The Magic Shoppe," "Cordelia's Choice," and "The News"; all of which won the Wordhaus Best Short Story Competition in 2013 and 2014, respectively. Desiree is also a Financial Aid Advisor at a prestigious law school in New York and an adult college student at SUNY Empire State College where she studies Creative Writing with a concentration in Cultural Studies. Her most important job is being the mother to a beautiful daughter, also known as the Warrior Princess, and the wife to an awesome husband. In her free time you can find her writing, reading romance novels, and tweeting. (thebklyntimes.blogspot.com)

Devyani Borade, Verbolatry: Devyani writes on the humor and pathos of everyday life. Her fiction, non-fiction, and art have appeared in magazines across the world. She likes to eat chocolates, read comic books, and try her husband's patience! (devyaniborade.blogspot.com)

Diane Stringam Tolley, **On the Border:** Diane was raised on one of the last of the large, old ranches in southern Alberta, Canada. She spends much of her time in the past remembering and recording the memories of the small, tow-headed little girl who was always getting into—and sometimes out of— scrapes. From fleeing disembodied chicken heads to dangling (quite literally) from a bull's tail, her escapades make for entertaining reading. Nowadays, Diane may be found at home in Beaumont, Alberta with her "husby" of thirty-eight years, surrounded by numerous children and grandchildren. A long-time journalist and author of countless articles and short stories, Diane has also penned numerous ebooks as well as two novels, *Carving Angels* and *Magic*. She blogs at On the Border. (dlt-lifeontheranch.blogspot.ca)

Jean Heffernan: Jean is a former teacher, aspiring chef, art history major, and aspiring photographer. She is constantly grateful to her parents and her student loans for funding her decade of indecision. She is currently staying at home with her two children, and although she has recently retired from blogging, she writes when she can. Jean is a contributor to the anthology *The HerStories Project.*

Jenny Kanevsky, In Other Words: Jenny lives in Austin, Texas with her two sons. Her novel, *Chosen Quarry,* is available on Kindle. She is a regular contributor at Huffington Post, The Good Men Project, and BLUNTmoms. Her work is also featured on Lipstick & Politics, Role Reboot, and What the Flicka?. You can follow her on Facebook and Twitter. She blogs at In Other Words. (jennykanevsky.com)

Jessica Azar, Herd Management: Jessica Azar, writes while raising four stair-step kids, known affectionately as The Herd, with her husband and college sweetheart in her Alabama hometown. She blogs at Herd Management and humorously details the adventures and mishaps of being a homeschooling, work-at-home-mom. She also happens to like running, and sipping Single Malt Scotch a whole lot. Jessica co-edited a mental health anthology entitled *Surviving Mental Illness Through Humor*, and has had essays published in humor anthologies like *Clash of the Couples*. She is a Huffington Post Blogger, POPSUGAR Select Blogger, a NickMom Ambassador/Writer and does marketing work for various prominent brands. Her published work can be read on POPSUGAR, Huffington Post, Scary Mommy, NickMom.Com, Venn Magazine, BluntMoms and other online locations. (herd-management.com)

Jessica Cantrell: Jessica Cantrell is the tired mother of two vivacious and well-freckled Irish girls. She finds solace in the woods, and in the musty breath of horses, and in her writing.

Kathryn Leehane, Foxy Wine Pocket: Kathryn Leehane is an American writer and humorist. She's penned essays ranging from ridiculously silly to heartbreakingly serious. One day she's recounting the horrors of her first (and last) Brazilian or explaining the finer points of farting "correctly" to her son, and the next she's grieving the pitfalls of friendship via Facebook.

Kathryn is also the voice behind the humor blog, Foxy Wine Pocket, where she shares twisted (and only sometimes exaggerated and inappropriate) stories about life as a mother, wife, friend, and wine-drinker in suburbia. She is a contributing author to several anthologies and is at work on her first book: a memoir about loss and survival. Her essays have also been featured on The Huffington Post, Erma Bombeck Writers' Workshop, Scary Mommy, and more.

Kathryn lives in the San Francisco Bay Area with her husband and two kids.

(foxywinepocket.com)

Kathy Radigan, My dishwasher's possessed!: Kathy is a writer, blogger, social media addict, mom to three, wife to one, and owner of a possessed appliance. She posts a weekly essay each Sunday on her blog, My Dishwasher's Possessed! which she started in the fall of 2010 after many doctors, teachers, and friends suggested that life with three children with a variety of learning issues (including a daughter with extensive special needs) might be of interest. Kathy has had her essays featured on the following online sites, What to Expect, Scary Mommy, Mamapedia, BlogHer, and The Erma Bombeck Writers' Workshop, among others. She is also a contributing author in two anthologies, *Sunshine After the*

About the Contributors

Storm: a survival guide for the grieving mother and *The HerStories Project: Women Explore the Joy, Pain and Power of Female Friendship.* She lives outside New York City with her family and still finds it hysterical that the woman who didn't even have an email address three years ago is now fully immersed in the online world. (mydishwasherspossessed.com)

Kristen Mae, Abandoning Pretense: Kristen is a devoted wife and mother, ADHD momma-warrior, violist, intermittent health-nut, and creator of Abandoning Pretense. Abandoning Pretense is a community where people are free to be honest about their struggles with marriage, parenthood, and life. Kristen's writing has been featured on Scary Mommy, BLUNTmoms, Mamapedia, Mamalode, Hot Mess Mom, and Good Men Project. (abandoningpretense.com)

Kristina Cerise, Defining Motherhood: Kristina is a Seattle writer, editor, and mom trying to find meaning in the madness. The mom she planned to be often shakes her head at the mom she has become. She caffeinates daily, blogs regularly, and tweets occasionally @DefineMother. (definingmotherhood.wordpress.com)

Lauren B. Stevens, lo-wren: Lauren is a freelance writer and blogger in Philadelphia whose work can be found on The Huffington Post, Scary Mommy, and Care.com. When she's not wrangling her toddler, you can find Lauren blogging about parenting and women's issues on her blog, lo-wren. (lo-wren.com)

Lea Grover, Becoming SuperMommy: Lea is a writer and speaker living on Chicago's south side. Her writing has been featured in numerous anthologies, including *Listen To Your Mother: What She Said Then, What We're Saying Now,* and on websites ranging from The Huffington Post to AlterNet to The Daily Mail Online. She speaks about sex positivity in parenting and on behalf of the RAINN Speakers Bureau. She can be found preparing her upcoming memoir or writing on her blog, Becoming SuperMommy.
(chicagonow.com/becoming-supermommy)

Linda Roy, elleroy was here: Linda is the wisecracking writer/musician behind the humor blog elleroy was here. She lives in New Jersey with her husband and two boys who swear she's the female Larry David. A 2014 BlogHer Voice of the Year for Humor, she is a regular contributor to The Huffington Post, and Humor Outcasts. Her work has been featured on numerous websites, including Scary Mommy, In the Powder Room, Erma Bombeck

Writers' Workshop, and BlogHer. She is co-author of several anthologies, including *I STILL Just Want To Pee Alone*, *Surviving Mental Illness Through Humor*, *The Bigger Book of Tweets*, *Clash of the Couples*; and *Only Trollops Shave Above the Knee*. Kvetch with her on Facebook, Twitter, Pinterest, Google+, Instagram; and laugh at her "musicomedy" on YouTube.

No wonder her family is always running out of clean underwear. (elleroywashere.com)

Lisa Carmody Doiron, Momologues-Soliloquies: Lisa lives in PEI, Canada with her husband and two boys. She blogs regularly at Momologues-Soliloquies on poop, barf and postpartum depression. Her stories have been featured on Mom Babble, What the Flicka?, and BLUNTmoms. When she's not writing, Lisa teaches music at a local public school. She's also part of a group of women lobbying government for better resources for mothers with postpartum depression in her province.
(elsiekarmadi.wordpress.com)

Lisa Webb, Canadian Expat Mom: In 2010, Lisa and her husband packed up their lives in Canada and moved to France. A few years and a couple of babies later, she's still bumping her way through the daily mishaps of becoming a mom in a foreign country. If laughter is the best medicine, this *Expat Mom* could open a pharmacy with the stories she's collecting on her overseas adventure. Lisa is the blogger behind Canadian Expat Mom and a regular contributor to BLUNTmoms and Parentdish Canada. (canadianexpatmom.com)

Lucia Paul, Dysfunctional Scrapbooking: Lucia Paul's humor-writing includes an award-winning sitcom script and essays that have appeared in numerous publications. Her parody, 50 Shades of Flannel, earned a cult following and was an Entertainment Weekly online Editor's Pick in 2012. She has been a regular humor contributor to *More* magazine's online edition, writing on topics ranging from the financial crisis to parenting teens. Her writing has also been featured on the Erma Bombeck Writers' Workshop, Midlife Boulevard, Better After 50, MinnPost, and numerous online communities. She is a contributor to several anthologies including *Not Your Mother's Book . . . On Home Improvement* and *Not Your Mother's Book . . . On Moms.* (dysfunctionalscrapbooking.blogspot.com)

Marcia Kester Doyle, Menopausal Mother: Marcia is a native Floridian, married, the mother of four children, and a grandmother. She is the author of the humorous blog, Menopausal Mother, where she muses on the good, the bad, and the ugly side of menopausal mayhem. Give her some wine and Nutella and she'll be your best friend. Marcia is a contributing writer at Huffington Post, What The Flicka?, In the Powder Room, and Humor Outcasts. Her work can also be found on Scary Mommy, BlogHer, Mamapedia, The Erma Bombeck Writers' Workshop, Lost in Suburbia, Better After 50, Generation Fabulous, Midlife Boulevard, and many others. She is the author of *Who Stole My Spandex? Midlife Musings from a Middle-Aged MILF* and a contributing author to *The Mother of All Meltdowns; Sunshine After the Storm;* and the *Life Well-Blogged* series. Marcia is a BlogHer Voice of The year 2014 recipient and her blog, Menopausal Mother, was voted Number One Top Comedy Blog 2014 at VoiceBoks as well as Top 25 in the Circle of Moms Contest 2013. (menpausalmom.com)

Mary Widdicks, Outmanned: Mary is the mom of two boys and a brand-new baby girl. She is also the owner of two male dogs. She spends the majority of her time trying to outsmart her kids (and she's failing at it). She used to be the only girl in the family and sometimes her voice got drowned out by fart jokes and belching contests. Once a cognitive psychologist, she turned to blogging and started Outmanned so she'd have a place to escape the testosterone and share her hilarious life with the rest of the world. Mary's writing has been featured on popular sites such as Mamapedia, Mamalode, Erma Bombeck Writers' Workshop, In the Powder Room, and Scary Mommy.

She is a regular contributor on BLUNTmoms and has been honored as a 2014 Voice of the Year by BlogHer as well as the Badass Blogger of the Year by The Indie Chicks. (outmannedmommy.com)

MD Marcus is a freelance writer and poet living in the past. Her profile articles can be found online in Simply Elevate Magazine and on PBSNet, and her poetry has been featured in the Red Dashboard Publishing anthology, *"dis-or-der,"* as well as in *Calliope Magazine*. (mdmarcus.com.)

Melissa Swedoski, Home on Deranged: After a career as a newspaper reporter and editor, Melissa thought she was well-informed on the chaos of everyday life. Then she married a man thirteen years her junior and became a stay-at-home mom to two toddler girls. Now she's mumbling through the mayhem of marriage and motherhood in a small Texas town, turning her investigative eye on the mishaps and misadventures of parenting and the marathon that is marriage, always with the emphasis on humor and love. She has a weekly column at Motherhood Later Than Sooner, and is in the anthology *The Mother of All Meltdowns*. She is "Tech Mom" on the Dallas TV show *The Broadcast*. You can find her living her big little life at her blog, HomeonDeranged.com.

About the Contributors

Michelle Grewe, Crumpets and Bollocks: Michelle is a former bookkeeper, airman, and office manager who is now a stay-at-home mother of three girls (PMS will be a bi*** someday) who drove her to a point of insanity, a place of no return (and even if there was a return, she wouldn't return it). She is a mom, monster hit man, bouncer, Twenty Questions master, semi-professional diamond thief, mad scientist, human jungle gym, and a terrible driver. Her addiction to Diet Coke, energy drinks, and random dancing has kept her functioning enough to appear sane to most of the world. She might be psychic, but if she is, she isn't psychic enough to know for sure. She is fascinated with mom bloggers, TS Eliot poems about cats, math, classical music, and hip-hop. In her spare time from plowing fields, she paints, blogs at Crumpets and Bollocks, plays piano badly dabbles in T-shirt design and "fontography." She is a walking paradox as she is the most intelligent idiot you will ever encounter. She is a scientific non-judgy Christian who loves love and peace. She knows it all because she admits she knows nothing. And her nonsense actually does make sense if you drink enough vodka and pray. (crumpetsandbollocks.com)

Michelle Matthews, Scattered Wrecks: Michelle is a graduate of George Washington University with a B.A. in Criminology, and her love of forensics has managed to seep into quite a few of her flash fiction pieces. A self-professed movie and TV snob, she also has an encyclopedic knowledge of all things musical. When she's not chasing twin toddlers and a kindergartener, she's blogging.

Her blog, Scattered Wrecks, showcases her short stories, social commentary, and advice. Her writing has been featured multiple times on BlogHer and Mamapedia. Michelle lives in northern Virginia with her three children. (scatteredwrecks.com)

Rachel Demas, The Tao of Poop: Rachel Demas spends her days with her delightful and frustrating three-year-old, Claire, in New York City. She blogs about the shock and amazement of being a first-time mom at The Tao of Poop. She has contributed writing to the anthology *The Mother of All Meltdowns* and is a contributing editor at Monkey Star Press, where she is currently working on the upcoming anthology *Mom for the Holidays* with two other contributing editors. (taoofpoop.blogspot.com)

Renea Dearing Dijab, thinkandponder: Renea is a liberal free-thinker currently living in Montgomery, Alabama. You can find her funny, true stories on her blog, thinkandponder. She produces a storytelling show called "Cheaper Than Therapy" at cheap-therapy-storytelling-show (dot) com. She lives with her husband, who has forbidden her to write about him (any more), and her daughter. (thinkandponder.com)

Sara Green, **MOTHERfluff:** Sara is the mom who isn't afraid to admit that her boys are annoying, gross, loud, and drive her to pour a bit more wine in her cup. Her house is often untidy, cluttered with toys and games, where beds go unmade, and floors are overdue for a cleaning. Sara tackles parenting with humor, confidence, and pragmatic realism. In creating her blog, MOTHERfluff, the process became a source of coping and comfort in battling post-partum depression after the birth of her youngest son and continues to be even more so while she recovers from an accident that left her bedridden for several months. Her therapy is sharing witty and offbeat stories that are realistic portrayals of *life as mom*. (motherfluff.com)

Sarah Almond, The Sadder But Wiser Girl: Sarah Almond is the anxious ADD Mother of two future Nobel Prize winners and the wife of one Evil Genius. Librarian by day, blogger late at night, she roams the cornfields of Iowa in search of dark chocolate, wine, all things caffeinated, and her car keys. She pens the wildly challenging blog The Sadder But Wiser Girl when she is not dabbling in other geekery. (thesadderbutwisergirl.com)

Shannon Day, Martinis and Motherhood, Tipsy Squirrel Press: Shannon is wife to one gorgeous, yet slightly overbearing, Brit; and mom to three little ladies. Once a teacher, now a story maker, and occasional cocktail shaker, she shares her tales, martinis, and her shenanigans over at Martinis & Motherhood. You can also find more of her writing on BLUNTmoms, In the Powder Room, Mamapedia, Scary Mommy, and Mamalode. Shannon is Co-founder of Tipsy Squirrel Press and Co-editor of the anthology/cocktail book: *Martinis & Motherhood: Tales of Wonder, Woe & WTF?!* Connect with Shannon on Facebook and Twitter. (martinisandmotherhood.com)

Shannon Drury, The Radical Housewife: Shannon is a writer, at-home parent, and feminist activist. Her memoir, *The Radical Housewife: Redefining Family Values for the 21st Century,* was recently published by Medusa's Muse Press. She lives in Minneapolis with her family. (theradicalhousewife.com)

Shannon Lell: Shannon was thrown from the corporate ladder in 2010. Shortly afterwards she started writing. Now, in between folding laundry and corralling two small children, she writes online at Shannon Lell and is the editor of Mamapedia.com. She has been featured in two anthologies, one obscure literary fiction journal, and numerous popular websites. She writes introspective pieces on personal and social issues, and she tries to use just enough sarcasm so you don't think she's emotionally unavailable. She also studies literary fiction at the University of Washington and is working on her first novel.

Over-thinking everything is her special super power. (shannonlell.com)

Shittu Fowora is a lifelong fan of history, and the power of scented words has recently been motivated by the winsomeness of birds and the wisdom of ants. Having been stung more than twice while attempting to lounge in trees to write verses, Shittu now spends more time around PCs ruminating, writing, and coding.

Stephanie Sprenger: Stephanie is a writer, editor, music therapist, and mother of two little girls. She blogs about the imperfect reality of motherhood at Mommy, for Real, and her work has been published on the Huffington Post, Mamalode, *Brain, Child Magazine*, and In the Powder Room, among other places. She was proud to be named one of BlogHer's 2014 Voices of the Year. As co-editor of *The HerStories Project*, she has published two books, with a third one—*Mothering Through the Darkness: Women Open Up About the Postpartum Experience*—to be released next fall by She Writes Press. She can usually be found behind her guitar, in front of her computer, or underneath a pile of laundry. She loves coffee, reading, yoga, and the Oxford comma, and her long-term goals include taming her neuroses and crafting the perfect witty bio. (www.stephaniesprenger.com)

T. Dawn Daum, W.T.F. words thoughts feelings: Dawn is momma to two little people. She relies on her sense of humor to keep her sane and her children alive. Dawn blogs at W.T.F. words thoughts feelings, and is co-editor of the anthology *Trigger Points: An Abuse Survivor's Experiences of Parenting.* (tdawneightyone.wordpress.com)

Tamara Woods, PenPaperPad: Tamara was raised (fairly happily) in West Virginia, where she began writing poetry at the age of twelve. Her first poetry collection, *The Shaping of an 'Angry' Black Woman*, was released in March of 2014. She has previous experience as a newspaper journalist, an event organizer, a volunteer with AmeriCorps and VISTA, and she has worked with people with disabilities. Tamara has used her writing background to capture emotions and moments in time for anthologies including *Empirical Magazine.* She is a contributing writer for the online 'zine *Lefty Pop;* and she writes articles as a full-time freelance writer. Tamara is a hillbilly hermit living in Honolulu with her "Mathmagician." (penpaperpad.com)

About the Contributors

Tina Parker: Tina grew up in Bristol, Virginia, and now lives in Berea, Kentucky, with her husband and two young daughters. Her full-length poetry collection entitled *Mother May I* will be published by Sibling Rivalry Press in 2016. To learn more about Tina, visit Tina-Parker.com.

Tracy Winslow, Momaical: Besides crafting cocktails with Zoloft, Tracy Winslow can be found cursing, crying into her coffee over her stretch marks, and Ouija-boarding her deceased metabolism. She was voted Top 25 Funniest Moms at Circle of Moms Pop Sugar, and Top 10 Funniest Moms on the Web by Parent Society. Tracy performed in Listen to Your Mother, is a featured writer for In the Powder Room, and contributor to the bestselling books *You Have Lipstick on Your Teeth* and *I Just Want to Pee Alone*—as well as seven other compilation books. When she's not trying to wrangle her children, she can be found teaching Spanish to high school students and blogging at Momaical.com.

Tricia Stream, Stream of the Conscious: Corporate writer by day, mommy blogger by night, Tricia is raising twin toddlers—Search and Destroy. Instead of having one baby after nine months, she had two after six; she's efficient like that. Tricia is a hybrid—running on coffee and chocolate. (streamoftheconscious.com)

Trish Hopkinson: Trish has always loved words—in fact, her mother tells everyone she was born with a pen in her hand. She has been published in several anthologies and journals, including *The Found Poetry Review*, *Chagrin River Review*, and *Reconnaissance Magazine*. You can follow her poetry adventures at TrishHopkinson.com.

Acknowledgements

Thank you to all the mom bloggers who have contributed to Moms Who Write and Blog over the years, without you, this anthology would have been a flashing light bulb.

A special shout out to Ana Manwaring: your expertise in the craft of writing (and editing) has been invaluable.

Our enormous appreciation to the best copy editor on the planet, Arlene Miller (you are the icing on the cupcake, make that one dozen cupcakes)!

A big thanks to our photographers, Michelle Lyman (that photo shoot in your bathtub was a blast), and Mr. and Mrs. Bill Bietler (thank you for the photos you took for our anthology project, all while you were sleep deprived, no doubt)!

Kudos to Lisa Knight of Designs Done Now for designing our book cover! Lastly, how can we forget Julie Maida of Next Life No Kids: you get credit for the title of the book, amaze balls!

About the Contributing Editors

Tina Bietler is a second-grade teacher and the blogger behind "The Busy Mom Guru" and "One Tired Working Mommy," where she deals with everyday issues from packing a healthy school lunch to dealing with ADHD, and even how to fake having clean hair so you can go to work. Writing has always been a love of hers. Tina has contributed to several "mommy" anthologies, and she has won an award from More Than Mommies for her blog, The Proper Way to Your Butt. She has written many fan fictions over the years under the pseudonym Kaitlyn Rose. Her dream is to write children's books as well as a novel *one day*. Married to her husband of seven years, she is mom to two rambunctious boys and one furry feline. Managing a classroom of thirty students while maintaining a home and family makes for days that are often busy, stressful, and exhausting, but thanks to Zoloft and a steady supply of wine, she can appreciate how truly blessed she really is. (onetiredworkingmommy.com)

Motherhood May Cause Drowsiness

Motherhood May Cause Drowsiness

Kristi Rieger Campbell is a semi-lapsed career woman with twenty years of marketing experience in a variety of national and global technology companies. While she does work part time, her passion is writing and drawing really stupid-looking pictures for her blog, Finding Ninee (pronounced *nine-ee* for her son's pronunciation of the word airplane). It began with a memoir about her special-needs son, Tucker, which Kristi abandoned after a publisher said she would rather shave a cat than read another memoir. Kristi has been featured on Autism Speaks, Scary Mommy, Mamapedia, and Families in the Loop, and was published in the popular anthologies *The HerStories Project, Mother of All Meltdowns, Awakening Wonder,* and *Life Well Blogged: Parenting Gag Reel.* She received a BlogHer's Voice of the Year People's Choice Award (category Exploration) and was a proud cast member of 2014 Washington DC's Listen to Your Mother Show. She almost always leaves the house in either flip-flops or Uggs, depending on the weather. (findingninee.com)

Lisa Nolan tags herself as "a supermom with a second-hand cape and an empty glass of wine." She's sported more occupations than she can count. At fifteen she sold trinkets on downtown street corners

{272}

in San Francisco (the city she was raised in by a single mom) and graduated to selling T-shirts to tourists.

She's done waitressing, retail, and daycare. She's been a college student, a writer (still), a Montessori teacher (twenty glorious years), a graduate student (English literature and creative writing), a literary magazine associate editor (*Flash Fiction*), a children's theater program director (the Marsh), a playwright, an underground comedy program director (The Mock Café), a theater manager (the Marsh), and a webmaster—until settling down to be a wife to a hard-working hubby (who still opens doors for her after twelve years), and a mom to a boy with Down syndrome.

She's suffered through fifteen years of chronic insomnia, the loss of her mom (while pregnant), functional alcoholism, depression, rage, the care of her addicted father (and the subject of her memoir, *Shoulders to the Trees*), countless meltdowns and panic attacks, and running after a wild monkey-boy day and night.

She became a mom blogger, an indie author, and a book editor. (And no, she never sleeps. And yes, she really is three people.) She resides in Northern California with her family: a chocolate Lab and two cats that get along superbly; an accidental watermelon patch; and a white-picket fence that always needs painting.

You can find Lisa Nolan herding cats and eating chocolate at Lisa Nolan (dot) com.

(lisanolan.com)

21427826R00173

Made in the USA
San Bernardino, CA
19 May 2015